BURT LANCASTER

Burt Lancaster

A Life in Films

Bruce Crowther

ROBERT HALE · LONDON

ISBN 0 7090 4349 X

Robert Hale Limited
Clerkenwell House
Clerkenwell Green
London EC1R 0HT

Photoset in Palatino by
Derek Doyle & Associates, Mold, Clwyd.
Printed in Great Britain by
St Edmundsbury Press, Bury St Edmunds, Suffolk
and bound by WBC Bookbinders Ltd, Bridgend, Glamorgan.

Contents

Illustrations

Between pages 64 and 65

Acknowledgements

The author is very grateful for the assistance and additional research of Dave Dalton. However, any factual errors which might occur are the author's sole responsibility, as are the opinions expressed herein.

Introduction

Growing old gracefully isn't easy for anyone. For a Hollywood actor blessed with youthful good looks and an athletic physique the difficulties of adapting to age multiply and few have managed the transition from handsome leading man to top-billed character actor. Burt Lancaster is one of that small number who successfully made the change.

In his early years in Hollywood his wide smile, rippling muscles and pantherlike grace of movement assured an audience for his films; his dedication to the craft of acting meant that in middle age he was able to effect the transition to character parts without discomfort; in old age, neither his looks nor his bearing had deteriorated markedly and he adjusted to patriarchal roles without causing embarrassment to those who remembered with affection his early appearances.

The role which launched Burt Lancaster's film career was that of 'Swede', the doomed pivotal character in director Robert Siodmak's *The Killers*. Few Hollywood actors can have begun their film careers so auspiciously, although many tried. Indeed, movie theatre screens of the immediate post-World War II years were littered with credit titles ending with the words: '... and introducing ...'.

Seen today, on late-night reruns on television, many of the actors so named are distinguished only by their obvious ineptitude and the speed with which their careers nosedived.

Burt Lancaster's first appearance was a long way from being inept; as for his career, that went rapidly up not down.

Seemingly unawed by the importance of his first screen role, Lancaster made a powerful physical impression which contrasted vividly with his controlled and underplayed acting. *The Killers* was a marvellous beginning and his immediate

Hollywood future was assured but, at thirty-three, Lancaster was old enough and smart enough (and had already experienced Hollywood's inability to know a good thing when it saw one) to know that he had a long way to go.

He also had the confidence, which some thought soon developed into arrogance, to know that he would make it to the top.

1   Starting Out

Burt Lancaster was born on 2 November 1913 in a tenement building owned by his parents at 209 East 106th Street in East Harlem. At the time, this part of New York City was home to a rich ethnic and religious mixture: Italians, Jews, blacks and many, like the Lancasters, from Northern European stock.

Burt's father, James H. Lancaster, an amiable and placid man, claimed descent from the English House of Lancaster, thereby displaying a not uncommon tendency among Americans to attempt to root themselves in Old World aristocracy. His mother was Welsh-Irish and had a fiery temperament overlaid with tactful generosity.

The Lancasters inherited the three-storey house in which they lived from Mrs Lancaster's father, and the rental income from several tenants was a welcome addition to Mr Lancaster's wages as a supervisor at Madison Square post office. The Lancasters were not, therefore, poor but neither were they well-off. Years later, Burt would recall that they 'never had enough clothing. People didn't then. You expected not to be quite warm enough in winter. But you simply ran to keep warm'.

When the Lancasters' fourth child was born they christened him Burton Stephen, having given his siblings the somewhat plainer names of James, William and Jane. (Another girl, Florence, was born after Burt but died in infancy.)

Despite his family's British ancestry, Burt's colouring, blue eyes and light blond hair, earned him the nickname 'Dutch'. (Among others who picked up the same and equally misapplied tag were the gangster Dutch Schultz, who was of German stock, and Dutch Reagan, the sports commentator turned actor and president, who claimed an Irish background.)

Burt grew slowly until his early teens and his small stature

11

made him the target of neighbourhood roughnecks but he quickly developed an ability to look after himself in such scrapes. Nevertheless, childhood acquaintances remember him as unaggressive and with few signs of the ferocious temper that would later strike fear into his co-workers in Hollywood.

Burt's scraps with other kids didn't leave a bad taste and in later years he looked back on his childhood as a time of happiness and neighbourly warmth. His home life was clearly one of love and contentment; it was also one in which standards and values played an important part.

His father's easygoing nature pushed the authoritarian role on to Burt's mother, who insisted upon strict adherence to a moral and respectable code of behaviour. When necessary, Mrs Lancaster could back up her homilies with a strong right arm and later references Burt made to his origins as 'black Irish' were reflected in his memories of his mother's temper. However, his father's placid nature impinged upon the boy and both parents' characteristics were mirrored in their youngest son's private and professional life ever afterwards.

As a small child, Burt enjoyed the applause of neighbours whenever he joined his father to sing outside the tenement on warm summer evenings. He sang in the church choir too and until his voice broke harboured a desire to become an opera singer. Indeed, even after it became clear that he could never sing professionally, it remained an idle dream and a lifelong regret.

As in so many New York immigrant communities, the church was a powerful influence, but religion never really took hold of the young boy and much later, when acting was his passion, he avoided religious roles until very late in life. The local church did, however, give him his first taste of theatre when, at the age of three, he appeared in a religious play.

Like many children of his generation, Burt went to the nickelodeon whenever he could afford it – or sneak in through a side door – and became a fan of Douglas Fairbanks, whose *Mark of Zorro* (1920), with its mixture of flamboyance, acrobatics and bravura acting, made an enormous impression upon him.

At thirteen, Burt began to grow quickly and just as swiftly ceased to be a target for the other kids on the block. Fights apart, there were endless opportunities to let off youthful steam. One such activity was swimming in the nearby river, but just how much Burt really enjoyed swimming is very doubtful. When he was older, he suffered from mild hydrophobia, which suggests that his youthful exploits were a display of his determination not to display fear and lose face with his peers: an early sign of an overwhelming inner drive which would not submit to hints of weakness.

Most of the growing boy's energies, both physical and intellectual, were taxed at the settlement house on East 104th Street. A settlement house was a kind of combined youth club, sports centre and educational unit for children in neighbourhoods otherwise deprived of such facilities. At the Union Settlement House, Burt took advantage of all activities offered: sports, music, art, languages and drama. These interests were not mere passing childhood fancies but remained with him into his adult life. With hindsight it can be seen that the most important of these activities were his dramatic ventures, which included amateur productions of former Broadway plays and tuition from members of the American Laboratory Theatre. The director of ALT was the Polish-born actor Richard Boleslawski, who had, in his turn, studied in Russia under Stanislavsky and directed films in Hollywood featuring such luminous stars as Greta Garbo, Charles Boyer and Marlene Dietrich, and in one, *Rasputin and the Empress* (1933), he had the considerable task of controlling the powerful talents of the three Barrymores, John, Ethel and Lionel.

Despite all the possibilities offered, Burt was not overly impressed with either acting or the theatre. When he heard that a talent scout was thinking of granting him an acting scholarship after seeing him portray a dying child in Booth Tarkington's *Three Pills in a Bottle*, he hid. Drama classes at the settlement house were not aiming towards a career; he saw them simply as a means of building up 'points' to ensure he went away to summer camp.

It was at one such camp that he met Nick Cravat, another young New Yorker whose home on East 108th Street was close to Burt's. The two became lifelong friends and later shared careers in two areas of show business. Nick was two years older than Burt and, despite his slight build, was as hard as nails. He fought professionally and by the time he was eighteen had clocked up almost as many bouts.

At the age of seventeen, Burt graduated from his local school,

PS83, and went to DeWitt Clinton High. Although not a model student he was an avid reader and perpetually scoured the shelves of the 110th Street public library. He also took every opportunity he could to listen to opera on the radio and even sneaked into the Metropolitan Opera House, just as he had done at the nickelodeon.

By now, Burt's physique had developed strikingly and his athletic ability gained him a basketball scholarship to New York University, where he excelled at sports, but was dissatisfied with the inadequate facilities for academic studies. Then, by chance, he saw an Australian gymnast practising at Union Settlement House and was immediately captivated by the athlete's display of strength and grace. Charles 'Curly' Brent was persuaded to teach Burt and Nick Cravat and two years later, in the spring of 1932, the two young men formed an acrobatic act.

Confident as only the young can be, they promptly quit school, bought an old car and went in search of work. Having read in the trades that the Kay Brothers Circus was on the road again after the winter, the two tyro entertainers, now calling themselves Lang and Cravat, decided to try their luck. They talked themselves into an audition where they did badly but somehow contrived to be taken on. For a joint wage of $3 a week they performed their act and helped out as riggers and handymen. After a month they were given a raise, but at the end of the summer Nick was injured and returned to New York. Burt was offered a job in another act but, realizing that this meant that his partner would never get back into the circus, he displayed a rare kind of loyalty and quit. When Nick recovered, the team of Lang and Cravat, their once amateurish skills now much refined, began working again in circuses, carnivals and at country fairs.

During 1935 Burt met June Ernst, an acrobat; they fell in love and were married. It was an impulsive decision and the marriage did not take. A few months later, Burt and Nick decided to return to New York while June remained on tour and the following year the young couple were amicably divorced.

Lang and Cravat's weekly rate of pay had risen to a very respectable $300 a week and they were soon working with the prestigious Ringling Brothers Circus. For all this great improvement over their tentative beginnings, Burt was becoming restless. He wanted something more but was unsure just what. He tried his hand at acting with the Federal Theatre Project (part of President Franklin D. Roosevelt's New Deal) but decided that he wasn't cut out for such work and rejoined Nick. Nevertheless, the theatre began to exert its influence upon him and during these years he went to shows whenever he was in New York.

He always remained somewhat reticent about his early brushes with the stage, as if embarrassed by the connotations of unmanliness some still attached to the profession, yet he could not help but be aware that the mid to late 1930s were a rich time for the American theatre and for New York in particular. Apart from Broadway there were the Federal Theatre Project, the American Laboratory Theatre and, in addition, Group Theatre, that extraordinary forcing-house of talent (and radicalism) in which flowered such talents as Lee J. Cobb, Frances Farmer, John Garfield, Elia Kazan and Clifford Odets. During this same period Burt saw Shakespeare on the stage for the first time when he attended a performance of *Hamlet* starring British actor, John Gielgud.

Meanwhile, Lang and Cravat tried their luck in vaudeville and clubs but their act was unsuitable for such venues and the limited world of the circus seemed to be the only place for them.

A trip to Los Angeles in 1939 allowed Burt to try the studios for film work, but he was turned down by executives unable to see beyond the acrobat's muscles. Had he been able to foresee the future he would doubtless have been amused to know that, one day, the successors of those myopic executives would fight for his name on a contract.

In 1941, on the way back east Burt suffered an injury, was forcibly laid off for a while, and decided that he'd had enough of circus life. While Nick Cravat continued a career as an acrobat, Burt Lancaster took on a succession of jobs.

In Chicago he worked at Marshall Fields' department store where he undertook such duties as floorwalker and salesman of shirts and ladies' lingerie. He alleviated the boredom of the first of these activities by performing acrobatics across the floor, while the second allowed him to exert his considerable physical charms upon the lady customers. While the staff enjoyed the former and the customers, presumably, the latter, the store's management were understandably disapproving and were not sorry when he decided to terminate his association with the company.

A series of jobs followed, all of which he thought of as dead-ended: fireman, engineer, domestic appliance repairman. He supplemented his earnings from these jobs by working as a singing waiter at a New Jersey nightclub but was then offered a post as salesman with CBS's Community Concerts Bureau. Not only did the job carry a salary of $6,000 a year, it was also in show business even if on the commercial side.

Burt approached the new job eagerly, seeing the link of selling and music as an ideal juxtaposition of those two sides of his personality: the brash extrovert and the musical dreamer. But this was 1942 and before he had time to settle in he was drafted. Unable to continue with CBS he spent the weeks before induction into the armed forces as singing waiter and comic's feed at a New York club, an omen for his new career in the military.

Later, Burt would refer to his time in the army with irritable disparagement. Although he volunteered for what he saw as 'real' duty, his showbiz background prompted the brass into assigning him to the Special Services branch of the Fifth Army where he was required to act, write and direct shows.

During the next two or three years he toured through North Africa, Sicily, Italy and Austria, occasionally rising to sergeant only to be busted back to private each time his temper placed him in conflict with any officer foolish enough to believe that rank outweighed experience.

The time he spent in Italy marked his first acquaintance with a country which would in time become a second home. It was also the place where he first met Norma Anderson.

Norma was a member of an all-girl act entertaining American troops. Norma, a widow with a year-old son, and Burt were immediately attracted and they became good friends. But this was still wartime and planning for the future made little sense, especially for Norma who had only recently lost her army-flyer husband.

In 1945, with the war over, Burt was back in New York awaiting his discharge and comfortably aware that his pre-war job with CBS was open to him. He had met up again with Norma, who had also returned to her old job, as secretary to Ray Knight, a radio producer with RCA in New York.

One day, when Burt was on his way to meet Norma at her office, he met a man named Jack Mahlor who was casting a Broadway-bound play. Coincidentally, the subject of the play concerned American GIs in Italy during the recently ended war. Mahlor asked Burt to audition for the role of Sergeant Joseph Mooney; he did and was offered the part. The only snag was that Burt must complete his final discharge before rehearsals began. With only hours to spare, he made it.

The play, *A Sound of Hunting* by Harry Brown, opened in Philadelphia for a two-week try-out before coming to Broadway in November 1945. Burt received good notices, as did Sam Levene and Frank Lovejoy who were also in the cast, but the play folded after three weeks in New York. The real war was too close for audiences to want reminding of it. (Seven years later, Hollywood turned the play into a movie, *Eight Iron Men*, with Lee Marvin in the role of Sergeant Mooney.)

Sam Levene, an experienced actor who had already made several films, saw latent talent in his theatrical comrade-in-arms and felt that he needed proper handling. Levene introduced Burt to Harold Hecht, then a struggling agent. The two men hit it off and Burt became a big fish in Hecht's pond, if only because he was almost alone in there.

Fortunately for both the actor and his new agent, Burt's performance in *A Sound of Hunting* had been seen by a number of talent spotters, including Hollywood producer Hal B. Wallis.

Wallis, who had been a prime mover in the rise of Warner Brothers, was sufficiently impressed to offer the actor a contract. Burt had been in show business of one kind or another for fourteen years, long enough not to be impressed by promises. He told Wallis to talk to his agent who was somewhat more impressed. Obviously Hecht knew how important and influential Wallis was; Burt had probably never heard of him.

The contract offered was for two films a year with options to make one more each year for other producers. It was a good deal for an actor; Burt Lancaster and Harold Hecht were already proving themselves to be nobody's fools.

In January 1946 Burt went to Hollywood where he was first

asked to read a scene from *A Sound of Hunting* for director Byron Haskin. 'Read' is not, perhaps, the right word. After rearranging the furniture in Haskin's office to simulate a foxhole, Burt delivered a performance that had staff in adjacent offices running for cover. He certainly impressed Haskin and a screen test was set up. The scene he played this time was from *Desert Fury*, a movie Wallis was planning to make.

Burt now displayed a sharp ear for Tinseltown rumour and gossip, and an equally sharp nose for business. He heard that journalist-turned-producer Mark Hellinger was having problems casting an important role in a movie he intended making from an Ernest Hemingway short story.

In addition to his hard-hitting journalism, Hellinger had written short stories and plays before becoming hooked on the movies. He worked on a number of Warner Brothers films of the 1930s, often under Hal Wallis's guiding hand, and *The Roaring Twenties* (1939) was based on upon some of his own experiences during Prohibition.

The Hemingway tale was *The Killers,* and Burt, who had read all the writer's work, craftily arranged for a member of Wallis's staff to screen his test for Hellinger. At a subsequent meeting, he acted as though he were the dumb 'Swede' the role demanded.

Hellinger offered him the role, at which point Burt dropped his act and revealed his awareness of the screenplay's shortcomings, offering some astute comments which proved his familiarity with the original material. Hellinger wryly conceded that he'd been fooled and that Burt Lancaster was nowhere near as dumb as he'd made out. Burt agreed that he was not.

Any mild duplicity on Burt's part was by now irrelevant: *The Killers* was in production, he was cast as Swede, and his second showbiz career was under way. This time, however, there was a difference. Unlike Lang and Cravat, who had begun at the bottom, Burt Lancaster was starting at the top.

2   Unlikely Icon

After he had abandoned his 'dumb Swede' impersonation for Mark Hellinger, Burt Lancaster had summed up Anthony Veiller's screenplay for *The Killers* (1946) by stating that 'the first sixteen pages are Hemingway verbatim and after that you have a rather interesting whodunnit film, but nothing comparable to Hemingway'.

He was right.

Veiller's screenplay begins by faithfully recording Ernest Hemingway's story of a murder carried out by two hired gunmen. This occupies little more than ten minutes of screen time, after which the script explores the reason, unstated by Hemingway, for the victim's passive acceptance of his fate.

The gunmen, Al and Max (Charles McGraw and William Conrad), arrive in the small town of Brentwood in the early evening. At a diner they ask about a man, known as the Swede, for whom they are searching. Making no attempt to conceal their malevolent interest, they obtain the Swede's address and leave. A young man from the diner, Nick Adams (Phil Brown), hurries to the rooming house where the Swede, who calls himself Peter Lunn, is living.

The Swede (Lancaster), his face hidden by shadows, is lying on his bed as Nick enters and urgently warns him about the two men.

'There's nothing I can do about it,' the Swede says.

'I can tell you what they look like,' Nick tells him.

'I don't want to know what they look like. Thanks for coming.'

'Don't you want me to go and see the police?'

'No. They wouldn't do any good.'

'Isn't there something I could do?'

'There ain't anything to do.'

'Couldn't you get out of town?'

'No, I'm through with all that running around.'

'Why do they want to kill you?'

'I did something wrong. Once. Thanks for coming.'

'Er, that's all right,' Nick says and leaves.

Alone, the Swede sits up, his face coming into the light for the first time. He listens, hearing the soft footfalls of the two gunmen as they mount the stairs. His expression displays not fear but resigned acceptance that his life is about to end. Maybe there is a hint behind the eyes that while he would not have willingly chosen to die in this way, death itself is not his enemy.

Moments later, the Swede dies in a hail of bullets.

This is where Hemingway's story ends, with no explanation of either the motive for the murder or the victim's unnatural refusal to avoid his murderers.

The film now explores both mysteries through the inquiries of an insurance investigator, James Riordan (Edmond O'Brien), whose company, Atlantic Casualty, is due to pay out a small policy on the Swede's life to a woman working as a cleaner at a cheap hotel in Atlantic City.

Riordan's investigation leads him to various undesirables who knew the Swede at different stages in his past. The Swede had been a professional fighter, then became a small-time crook, and was eventually a participant in a big payroll robbery. These events, portrayed in flashback, show how the Swede, in common with many *film noir* heroes, had fallen under the spell of a beautiful but evil woman.

The woman, Kitty Collins (Ava Gardner), draws the Swede, whose real name is Ole Andreson, into a web of cross and double-cross after the successful payroll heist. Kitty tells him that the rest of the gang plan to cheat him out of his share of the loot and urges him to beat them to it and run away with her. In reality, Kitty is hand-in-glove with Jim Colfax (Albert Dekker), the brains behind the robbery. It is they who plan to take the money for themselves but need a fall guy and the Swede, dumbly infatuated with Kitty, is perfect for the frame.

Later, on the lam in Atlantic City, the Swede is left flat when Kitty disappears with the money. With the rest of the gang intent on recovering the loot, and on vengeance for his betrayal, the Swede, now broke and broken-hearted (but briefly befriended by the woman who cleans his room), changes his name and hides out in Brentwood where he takes a job at a motor repair shop.

One day, Colfax chances to drive through Brentwood and comes face to face with the Swede. Colfax knows that sooner or later another member of the gang will also happen to come this way and when they see the Swede's obvious poverty it will be but a short step to conclude that Colfax must be the real betrayer. Colfax knows that he must eliminate his fall guy and the Swede knows it too. Worse for the Swede is the fact that he knows his death will be the final act in his doomed, one-sided love affair with Kitty.

Insurance investigator Riordan is now working with police lieutenant Sam Lubinsky (Sam Levene, who had introduced Burt Lancaster to Harold Hecht), a childhood friend of the Swede's. Lubinsky had married the Swede's former sweetheart, Lilly (Virginia Christine), and continually displays feelings of guilt at his role in the Swede's life. He even arranges for the body to be shipped back from Brentwood for burial, paying the expenses himself.

Riordan and Lubinsky sort out the tangled web by pursuing all leads to former contacts of the dead man, only one of whom, Charleston (Vince Barnett), a drunk who once shared a prison cell with the Swede, is a halfway decent character. During their joint incarceration, and using the stars as an analogy, Charleston tried to show the Swede the futility of reaching for the unreachable. The lesson didn't stick.

Charleston is lucky in one respect: his contact with Riordan brings only a skinful of booze. Others are less fortunate. Two former gang members, Blinky and Dum Dum (Jeff Corey and Jack Lambert), wind up dead. Dum Dum's last act is fatally to wound Colfax who dies at Kitty's feet unable to respond to her plea to clear her of complicity.

As Lancaster had predicted, from the moment Anthony Veiller's screenplay takes over from Hemingway's short story and explores new ground, the film undergoes a shift of emphasis. Good as the whole film is, the later sequences never come up to the brilliant opening. The superb shadowed photography of Woody Bredell, the casual menace of the killers, the oblique hard-boiled dialogue that is almost pure Hemingway, all blend to from a perfect evocation of the essence of *film noir*.

The rest of the film is partly the story of a man's doomed and ultimately fatal love for a heartless and ruthless woman; partly a caper movie which proves in passing that there is no honour among thieves; partly a cops and robbers thriller. In all departments *The Killers* works extremely well, even if some of the high hopes invoked by those first ten minutes are never quite realized.

The director of *The Killers*, Robert Siodmak, began his film career in Germany working first in silent movies alongside such fellow countrymen as his brother Curt, Edgar Ulmer, Billy Wilder and Fred Zinnemann, all of whom also moved to Hollywood. Siodmak's own departure for the film capital came in 1940 when he was working in Paris; he left just a few steps ahead of the Nazis.

Siodmak was among the German expatriate film-makers responsible for the development of what would eventually become known as American *film noir*. He helped to bring to essentially American stories in uniquely American settings the grim and often morbid visual imagery of German Expressionist cinema. He also brought new angles on old ideas. In *The Killers*, one of Siodmak's best films, he shows the robbery of the Prentiss Hat Factory in one long single-take sequence. It is a masterly accomplishment and would have been the high point in any one of a score of contemporary thrillers. It is a measure of the tension of those opening moments in the Brentwood diner and rooming house that here the robbery's impact is substantially lessened.

Cinematographer Woody Bredell's moodily evocative work was a hallmark of other *films noirs*, including *Lady on a Train* (1945), a rare *noir* comedy which starred Deanna Durbin; the Claude Rains *tour de force*, *The Unsuspected* (1947); and two other films with Siodmak, *Christmas Holiday* and *Phantom Lady* (both 1944).

Among the other leading roles in *The Killers* Ava Gardner fares best as the *femme fatale* with Albert Dekker less than convincing either as the brains or as Gardner's lover. Edmond O'Brien and Sam Levene do well enough given that their parts call for them mainly to carry the narrative. Fortunately, most of the supporting roles are well played with the opening sequence being enhanced by gravelly-voiced Charles McGraw and rotund William Conrad (long before he followed his enormous waistline into the television series *Cannon*).

Lancaster's interpretation of Ole Andreson, the dumb Swede plunged into emotional turmoil beyond his control or comprehension, is masterly. It is difficult to imagine many of his contemporaries having the ability to portray a man of such soft vulnerability without tipping over into bathos. Certainly none of those who might have had the acting talent the role demanded was also equipped with the physical build required to play the part of a prizefighter (Mark Hellinger's original thoughts on casting included Wayne Morris and Sonny Tufts, neither of whom possessed a fraction of Lancaster's screen presence nor, as it turned out, his acting skills).

By whatever standards are applied, Lancaster's is an impressive début, blending physical power and masochistic resignation, and this performance still stands among his finest. His enormous self-confidence clearly lifts him over a few tricky passages, while his wide experience of performing in public gave him an important edge, even if nothing that he had done before was directly linked to the special requirements of film-making.

Nevertheless, critic Bosley Crowther, whose occasionally sledgehammer wit was currently being used to lambaste Robert Mitchum and other supposedly dumb hunks, was noticeably 'underwhelmed' by Lancaster's performance, remarking in the *New York Times* that 'a new actor, Burt Lancaster, gives a lanky and wistful imitation of a nice guy who's wooed to his ruin'.

Other reviewers were more encouraging: Otis L. Gurnsey Jr in *The New York Herald-Tribune* referred to 'a most promising screen début' while Harris Deans in London's *Sunday Times* said 'I have a feeling we're going to see more of Burt Lancaster.'

Deans was right and already producers were scrambling for Lancaster's services. The irony of these suddenly opened doors did not escape the actor who had knocked unavailingly at many of them seven years earlier. Neither can he have missed seeing how good luck plays a part in an actor's career. If he hadn't persuaded Mark Hellinger to take a chance on him his first screen role would have been in *Desert Fury*, a film which, despite the fact that Hal Wallis had ordered hasty rewrites to boost Lancaster's role, was a decidedly inferior vehicle.

After working on *The Killers* Lancaster was asked to appear on Broadway in the original production of *A Streetcar Named Desire*. The leading role of Stanley Kowalski had first been offered to John Garfield but when problems arose the part was offered to Lancaster. In an interview with Gordon Gow in *Films and Filming*, Lancaster commented upon the unfortunate fact that a film commitment prevented him from taking up the offer, which was made with the enthusiastic backing of both the author, Tennessee Williams, and the director, Elia Kazan. In the event the role went to the third choice, Marlon Brando. It is idly speculative, but nevertheless intriguing, to consider the effect upon Lancaster's career had he played Kowalski, and the effect on Brando's had he not.

The success of Lancaster's film début and the promise the future held gave a sense of stability to his life – something which had been notably lacking in the past. It was in this atmosphere that he and Norma Anderson decided to marry, the ceremony taking place in Yuma, Arizona, on 28 December 1946.

After living for a while at Malibu Beach, the Lancasters moved into Bel-Air and a house big enough to accommodate a large and growing family. Apart from Burt and Norma there was James Stephen, Norma's son from her first marriage, Burt's brother James, now his legal adviser, his parents (his father acted in a quasi-managerial role) and, in 1947, his and Norma's first child, William Henry. The large household was quite a drain on his suddenly substantial earnings and, as he once remarked to Mark Hellinger, 'You know, I don't seem to have any money.'

For all the outgoings, however, Lancaster's income rapidly set him on the way to becoming a rich man although he did not act like one. While he might have indulged his appetite for music and art, he and Norma lived modestly (the palatial Bel-Air house apart), generally avoided the party-going crowd, and he quickly built a reputation as one of Hollywood's worst-dressed men.

Lancaster made a guest appearance in *Variety Girl* (1947), along with a dozen or so stars making cameo appearances, and was then hard at work with Hellinger, who knew a good thing when he saw one, on another starring role.

Hollywood regularly used the tightly enclosed world of the

penitentiary as a setting for high drama and *Brute Force* (1947) is one of the better efforts.

Fully living up to its title, the film is uncompromising in its depiction of violence by jailers against prison inmates and the equal savagery with which the convicts eventually respond.

Under the sadistic eyes of Captain Munsey (Hume Cronyn), the prison guards brutalize their charges to the point where the prisoners have no choice, short of allowing themselves to be reduced to the level of animals, but to fight back.

Just like the gangster-movie genre, prison films rarely made heroes out of the enforcers of law and order – instead cheerfully, if misguidedly, granting hero status to a succession of dyed-in-the-wool villains. This rarely happened in a reformist mood but arose almost accidentally from the fact that cast in the roles of guards were unknown character actors while the meaty roles of the prisoners went to stars like Humphrey Bogart, James Cagney and Edward G. Robinson.

Driven to extremities, the convicts in *Brute Force*, led by Joe Collins (Lancaster), hatch an escape plot with the help of Gallagher (Charles Bickford), an old lag respected by most of the other convicts. The cons' plans are in danger of being revealed to Munsey through an informer, Wilson (James O'Rear), but this source of information is unpleasantly eliminated when blowtorch-wielding fellow-inmates dispatch Wilson under a drop hammer in the prison workshop.

With his informer thus wafered, the guard captain steps up the offensive against the cons but a diversion planned by Gallagher enables Collins and his comrades to attempt his doomed break-out. By the inevitable end few of the principals on either side of the fence have survived, with Collins dying from gunshot wounds after tossing Munsey from one of the prison's towers.

The terse screenplay, in which violence and corruption are seen as normal human characteristics, is the work of Richard Brooks. Among the film's flaws are the one-sidedness of the characterizations (at one point Munsey has a prisoner beaten, the hapless victim's cries of pain drowned by Wagner thundering from a phonograph) and a succession of flashbacks which show the prisoners' lives before their incarceration. Hollywood dictated such moments as a means of bringing light relief into the darkness of the pen, to open up the static nature imposed by prison walls, and, of course, as a means of putting a few women in front of the cameras in what was otherwise an all-male setting. Fortunately, on this occasion the damage to the film's narrative flow such diversions threaten is largely overcome by strong direction from Jules Dassin.

Dassin's promising career in America came to an abrupt halt after a trio of successes – *Brute Force, The Naked City* (both 1948) and *Thieves' Highway* (1949) – when he fell foul of the House Un-American Activities Committee. Forced to work in Europe, he made the best 'British' *film noir, Night and the City* (1950), before moving to the Continent to direct the remarkable *Rififi* (1955), which spawned a thousand cardboard-copy caper movies, and the much underrated *He Who Must Die* (1957).

For Lancaster, *Brute Force* was an opportunity to build upon the doomed character he had played in *The Killers*. Although similarly unable to avoid his destiny, Joe Collins is a much more positive character than the Swede, and while the storyline makes his fate inevitable he has none of his predecessor's resignation and self-destructive vulnerability.

Bosley Crowther, in the *New York Times*, was still unimpressed by the star, commenting merely that 'big-framed, expressionless Burt Lancaster gives the chief convict a heroic mold', saving his enthusiasm, such as there was, for the film's director.

For all such critical disdain, the role of Joe Collins capitalized upon Lancaster début performance as Ole Andreson, removed any doubts there might have been that he was a one-shot wonder and established him as an actor with undeniable star quality. It also ensured that for a while he teetered on the edge of being typecast with a number of roles in *films noirs*, despite the fact that, outwardly at least, he bore none of the characteristics of other *noir* icons currently in vogue in Hollywood (like Humphrey Bogart, always a dubious choice, and Robert Mitchum, the genuine article).

The film for which Lancaster had made his original screen test came next, but although *Desert Fury* (1947) was the star's first colour film it had little else to brighten it.

When Paula Haller (Lizabeth Scott) returns home to Arizona she takes up with gambler Eddie Bendix (John Hodiak). Their romance meets with local disapproval, especially from deputy sheriff Tom Hanson (Lancaster) who knows that something nasty lurks in Eddie's past. Eddie Bendix's partner, Johnny (Wendell Corey), is also displeased at Paula's influence over the gambler. It is Johnny who urges Paula's mother, Fritzi (Mary Astor), who owns the local gambling joint and hopes for better things for her daughter, to tell Paula how Eddie's wife died in a mysterious car accident probably engineered by her less than loving husband. Convinced at last, Paula makes a run for it. Eddie shoots Johnny, chases after Paula, and accidentally drives his car over the same bridge where his wife became his widow.

Lancaster's role during all this hectic activity is rather passive even though, as he later told Gordon Gow in *Films and Filming*, Hal Wallis reworked the script to accommodate the fact that he now 'had a star on his hands'. Even so, he does well enough with a predictable screenplay filled with inadequately developed characters. Of his fellow actors, Wendell Corey, in his first screen role, comes off best with a sound, tight-lipped performance while Arizona looks beautiful.

The lightweight nature of *Desert Fury* was countered by Lancaster's next role. Another *film noir* entry, *I Walk Alone* (1948), tells a not unfamiliar tale of two gangsters whose partnership is disrupted when one goes to prison taking the rap for a joint venture beyond the law. When the convict comes out he expects to pick up his share, but his confident if naïve expectations are not met. There is seldom honour among thieves, as any ticket buyer in movie theatres everywhere could have told him.

The betrayed gangster in *I Walk Alone* is Frankie Madison and his double-crossing partner is Noll Turner (Kirk Douglas, with whom Lancaster formed one of his few off-screen friendships with actors, and one which was to last). The gangsters' differences are accentuated by the nature of their criminality. Turner, now deeply involved in organized crime, closely resembles the acceptable image of the corporation executive; Madison is a relic from a bygone age of crime when, or so this film would have us believe, a criminal could also be an honourable man. Hollywood's crime movies are liberally peppered with these quasi-Robin Hood figures, reflecting the near-reverence with which many Americans viewed the vicious and unprincipled gangsters of the bootleg era, a false judgement which has ever since damaged much of public life.

Frankie Madison's response to his former partner's duplicity is muted until his brother Dave (Wendell Corey) is murdered. No longer prepared to be stepped on, Madison goes on to the offensive and avenges his brother's death at Turner's considerable expense. Unwilling to live in this new criminal world of which he can never be a part, Madison goes straight and even gets the girl, Kay (Lizabeth Scott), who was one of the perks provided by Turner to keep his partner preoccupied.

Although within the flexible framework of *film noir*, *I Walk Alone* contains many elements that weaken its claim for such classification. The director, Byron Haskin, in whose office Lancaster had re-enacted a scene from his Broadway play, had had a varied career making westerns, thrillers, adventure yarns, all with considerable visual *élan*, a by-product of his complementary career as a cinematographer. But his general competence was not particularly well suited to the special and quirky requirements of *film noir*, and *I Walk Alone*, his only venture into the category, contains idealistic overtones that sit uneasily with the more appropriately downbeat moments. The extensive use of popular songs of the day (Kay is a nightclub singer) adds to the uneasiness. Jazz was the only musical form which ideally suited the ambience of *film noir*.

Although Lancaster has a much less commanding role than in either *The Killers* or *Brute Force* he nevertheless dominates the film (this was before Kirk Douglas had developed his own brand of screen-stealing acting). The moviegoing public was thus given further evidence of a burgeoning box-office talent.

I Walk Alone was based upon Theodore Reeves's stage play *Beggars are Coming to Town* but its theatrical origins are not particularly obvious, unlike Lancaster's next film which was an adaptation of an Arthur Miller play.

All My Sons (1948) co-stars Lancaster with Edward G. Robinson and Howard Duff (who had made his screen début with Lancaster in *Brute Force*) in the story of an industrialist tried and acquitted for selling the government dangerously defective components for airforce planes.

It is a highly concentrated dramatic exercise in family conflicts over differing concepts of loyalty. The industrialist, Joe Keller (Robinson), edges the blame on to his partner, Henry Deever (Frank Conroy), and it is the partner's daughter, Ann (Louisa

Horton), who tells Chris Keller (Lancaster) the truth. Chris is appalled by the fact of his father's duplicity, which is brought dreadfully home by the realization that among the victims of the fraud is his (Chris Keller's) own brother who, knowing the truth, deliberately flew to his death as an act of atonement for his father's guilt. Chris exposes his father and in the process reveals the truth about his brother's death, an act which leads to Joe's suicide.

This was heady stuff on the stage. Transferred to the screen, some of the original's intensity is retained as is a suitably claustrophobic setting, but the overall effect is an impression of immobility. The static nature of *All My Sons* was unattractive to those who favoured the more usual vitality of film and contributed to the muted response of audiences.

Nevertheless, Lancaster (who had seen the play on Broadway) in common with the others who worked on the film, must be credited with working at less than the usual rate in order that the film should be made at all. This attitude towards material which fell outside the mainstream of Hollywood movies was one that Lancaster would always retain and would soon back wholeheartedly.

Among Lancaster's colleagues on the film was Mady Christians (in the role of Kate Keller), a fine stage actress who fell foul of McCarthyism and, faced with the bleak prospect of being unable to work because of her political beliefs, took her own life.

Lancaster's performance in the film is effective but not outstanding, with Eddie Robinson, in the meatiest role, confidently taking the acting honours. Nevertheless, Robinson was impressed by Lancaster, observing in his autobiography, *All My Yesterdays*, that the younger man was already 'showing that animal vitality and suppressed violence inside that inevitably made him a star'.

Undoubtedly, Lancaster was delighted at this first opportunity to play a role with deep philosophical undertones. Already, he was becoming highly critical – and outspokenly so – of the stories upon which many films are based. In time this would approach the level of an obsession and, indeed, he had already expressed doubts over Hal Wallis's literary standards – criticism which ignored the fact that the producer was not in business to create works of art but rather to keep his eye and ear keenly attuned to what led to box-office success.

The 'staginess' of *All My Sons* was repeated in Lancaster's next film but this time claustrophobia was an essential ingredient. *Sorry, Wrong Number* (1948) was adapted by Lucille Fletcher from her own internationally acclaimed radio play, a tightly written essay on self-instilled fear. In this gripping little drama, the fear ultimately but too late proves to be fatally justified.

Leona Stevenson (Barbara Stanwyck) is a rich invalid who aggressively dominates her meek husband, Henry (Lancaster). The telephone is Leona's only contact with the outside world and one night, on a crossed line, she overhears two men plotting a murder. She calls the police but they don't believe her interpretation of what she has heard; even if they did, there is nothing they can do as a chance eavesdropping cannot be traced.

Angry at official indifference, Leona pursues the matter herself and is horrified to discover not only that she is the potential victim but also that her henpecked Henry is one of the plotters.

Henry Stevenson has allowed himself to be pressurized into an arrangement with a blackmailer named Moreno (William Conrad) who will kill Leona, thereby allowing her husband to inherit her estate. All goes well with the plan until Henry, who thought he was merely hastening his wife's imminent demise, discovers that Leona's illness is not terminal, as he had believed, but is in fact psychosomatic. Too late, he changes his mind and tries to warn her; he hears her scream over the phone before Moreno's voice tells him he has a wrong number. Arrested by the police, who have begun to take a belated interest in the case, Henry ends as he began – an ineffectual loser.

Sorry, Wrong Number is one of a tiny handful of *films noirs* which feature a woman in the central role. Doomed from the outset, which thus places her on common ground with other *noir* characters, Leona's fate is inextricably linked with that of Henry – a fact which joins them closer than was ever the case in their loveless marriage. While he may cause her death, the manner in which she has acted towards him makes her the architect of her own demise.

Barbara Stanwyck is undoubtedly the star of the film. An

actress of consistently high quality throughout her long career, Stanwyck turned in one fine performance after another and was acclaimed by her colleagues as a solid, hard-working and untemperamental professional.

This was the first time Lancaster gave the kind of unstinting and unselfish support a female co-star needed to bring in a bravura performance. It was not to be the last, and later examples of this kind of professional generosity would result in Academy Awards for the two fortunate women concerned. Stanwyck was not so lucky and although nominated for an Oscar for *Sorry, Wrong Number* and for three other movies during her career it was an award she never won. Her peers helped set this injustice straight in 1982 by granting her a special Oscar for her services to the motion-picture industry.

One result of the interchanging of male/female roles in *Sorry, Wrong Number* is that Lancaster is left with the softer, more feminine character. While his role as the morally inadequate husband bears a few surface similarities to his other *noir* roles, it is well removed from either the masochistic Swede or the hard-nosed Joe Collins.

Lancaster had been obliged to press hard to be allowed to make this film (as he had with *All My Sons*) and to some extent Hal Wallis's reluctance was mirrored by audiences, which were a little uneasy with this shift of character; but, importantly for his career, it was a part which allowed him to develop his craft and prove his worth as an actor of subtlety in a decidedly passive role.

His good intentions cut no ice with Bosley Crowther, writing in the *New York Times*, who finally threw off all restraint and hammered Lancaster's interpretation of Henry Stevenson as being 'a painfully obtuse performance'.

Unmoved by such criticism, Lancaster tackled another *noir* role, but one which gave him a much greater piece of the action even if the film was inferior to his earlier essays in the genre.

Despite its title (or perhaps because of it) *Kiss the Blood off My Hands* (1948) is a considerable disappointment.

Set in London (but filmed in Hollywood), the story follows Bill Saunders (Lancaster) from the moment when, in a fit of anger, he kills the landlord of a pub. On the run from the police, Bill meets up with Jane Wharton (Joan Fontaine), a nurse, and Harry

Carter (Robert Newton), a small-time crook. Carter was a witness to the killing and uses this hold it gives him to draw Bill into his own nefarious schemes.

Imprisoned on another charge, Bill is eventually released and takes a job as a truck driver at the hospital where Jane works. Carter turns up again and blackmails Bill into stealing drugs. Unwillingly, Bill agrees but changes his mind when, on the night of the planned robbery, Jane has to make the trip with him.

Carter than tries to blackmail Jane into providing drugs, threatening to tell the police about Bill. When Jane refuses to bow to his threats Carter attacks her and she kills him in self-defence. Bill and Jane decide to leave the country, but at the last moment he undergoes a change of heart. Knowing that they can have no kind of life together, Bill gives himself up and confesses to the murder of the pub landlord. With the whole story told, the way is clear for Jane to prove that her killing of Carter was justifiable homicide.

Generally unsatisfactory in most departments, the film was a particular disappointment to those drawn in by the extravagant title. Lancaster's co-stars are not at their best: Joan Fontaine, always a subdued performer, was pregnant at the time and Newton, who revelled in over-the-top parts, is clearly uneasy. Lancaster gives a satisfactory performance of a complex character (but cannot escape the persistent masochism which followed him through the world of *film noir*, and suffers a flogging during his short spell in prison), but his best scenes – those in which he flits through the darkened city – really belong to cinematographer Russell Metty.

At this stage of his career, Burt Lancaster was already wearying of the manner in which Hollywood dictated the paths upon which actors were supposed to travel. Intent upon controlling his own career, he turned himself into a corporation, Norma Productions, and he and Harold Hecht had also formed an independent production company, Hecht–Norma. Inauspiciously, *Kiss the Blood off My Hands* was their first venture but they had their sights firmly set on better things, and better things duly came their way.

In the mean time, he had an outstanding commitment to fulfil. He and Robert Siodmak were contracted to make another film,

Criss Cross (1949), with Mark Hellinger but were dispirited by the producer's sudden death at the age of forty-four. Partly through their respect for the dead man and partly because their contracts had passed to Hellinger's estate, which now was owned by his widow, they went ahead. Unfortunately, control of the film was now in the hands of Universal Studios, which ordered a rewrite, resulting in what Lancaster told Gordon Gow was a 'rehashed chow of a script'.

In *Criss Cross* Lancaster takes the role of Steve Thompson, a security guard who is recently divorced and struggling with a drink problem. He still carries a torch for his ex-wife Anna (Yvonne De Carlo) but she is now hooked up with gangster Slim Dundee (Dan Duryea).

Not surprisingly to *aficionados* of the genre, Steve is soon enmeshed emotionally with Anna and criminally with Dundee. After helping set up a robbery against his own organization, Steven is shot and wounded by the gang, which kills one of his fellow guards. In retaliation, Steve kills two of the gang and is acclaimed a hero even though the money is gone.

Pete Ramirez (Stephen McNally), a friend of Steve's, is the detective assigned to the case and is uncertain of the truth of the story, especially as Anna has now disappeared. Meanwhile, Slim Dundee, angry at the death of two of his men and the fact that he has no idea where the money is hidden, has Steve kidnapped from his hospital bed. The wounded man persuades his abductors to take him to Anna, unwittingly pointing Dundee there too.

Steve's arrival at Anna's hide-out, where she is keeping herself amused by counting the loot, causes her to make a run for it, unhesitatingly abandoning him to his fate. But she is killed by Dundee who also murders Steve before being cornered by the pursuing police.

Director Siodmak again drew from his star a performance of subtly controlled power and neither Lancaster's weariness at his cycle of doomed, masochistic heroes, nor their joint reluctance to continue with the film after Mark Hellinger's death shows through.

However, the real star of *Criss Cross* is cinematographer Franz Planer, who sets the mood from the opening scenes of the city by night. Although making more use of full-lit scenes than is usual in many *films noirs*, the quality of such moments is not allowed to undercut the prevailing mood. Indeed, Siodmak's and Planer's conception is such that even these brightly lit scenes fit into the overall mood by their implied contrast with the seediness of the milieu in which much of the rest of the action takes place.

Czechoslovakian by birth, Planer worked extensively in German silent cinema before moving to Hollywood, where he worked with Max Ophüls on a number of films including *Letter from an Unknown Woman* (1948). Planer's range was broad and he worked in several European countries including Britain. Among his many American credits were *Champion* (1949), which made a star of Kirk Douglas, *Death of a Salesman* (1951), *The Caine Mutiny* (1954), *The Big Country* (1958) and *Breakfast at Tiffany's* (1961).

Critical reactions to *Criss Cross* were varied. In Bosley Crowther's absence from the *New York Times*, a reviewer lurking behind the initials T.M.P. was unsure if the star had overcome the problems of typecasting. 'Burt Lancaster eventually gets around to being the same old tough guy as of yore. It should not be surprising that his performance is competent, for he has been working at the same type of role for some time.'

Lancaster would not have argued with the implied criticism for it matched his own view of his work at this time; but the cycle was not yet over. Although his next film was outwardly an open-air adventure story, his role bore many similarities to other characters he had portrayed.

Rope of Sand (1949) was designed by Hall Wallis to capitalize upon the success of *Casablanca* a few years earlier by rounding up the usual character players including Peter Lorre, Paul Henreid and Claude Rains. The concoction didn't work a second time, which was more unfortunate for Wallis than anyone, because this movie marked the end of the contract he had with Lancaster, who had no reason to back away from his determination to go his own way in future.

For all the comparative disappointment of his recent films, this was anything but an unhappy time for Lancaster. His personal standing in Hollywood was unassailable even if his massive self-confidence was such that he regularly argued with film-makers more experienced than he about the manner in which they should do their work.

Domestically, he was even more settled, with the birth of a daughter, Susan Elizabeth, in 1949 acting as further reinforcement to his seemingly unbreakable relationship with Norma.

The end of the decade found him able to look back contentedly on starring roles in nine feature films. Even if some had been lightweight, his technical competence was never in doubt. In *The Killers*, *Brute Force*, *Sorry, Wrong Number*, and even in the less successful *Criss Cross*, he was excellent and had more than justified his instant accession to starring roles in major productions.

More important to Lancaster himself was the fact that these films proved his ability as an actor. Perhaps the range was somewhat limited but this had the advantage of giving him an opportunity to refine his new craft on known territory, even if that meant carving a temporary niche as a rather improbable, doomed masochist.

In fact, his physical unsuitability for such roles enhanced his performances, providing as it did a striking contrast to the muted, soft-spoken interpretations he gave. This appearance of great physical strength surrounding a soft and vulnerable core made his characters' almost psychotic determination to lose at all costs acceptable to audiences which might have reacted rather differently to, say, Humphrey Bogart or James Cagney in such roles.

More than any other *film noir* hero, Lancaster drew upon an ability to project the soft masochistic vulnerability of an outwardly tough, dangerous and potentially violent man. Masochism is uncharacteristic of *noir* heros and it helped provide the genre with one of its least likely icons.

It is a measure of the quality of Lancaster's acting ability that he could now reverse these characteristics to show with equal conviction men who were outwardly gentle yet possessed an inner core of sprung steel.

The 1950s would provide many opportunities to test these alternative skills as he began to develop the range of his craft. It would prove to be a much wider range than anyone – himself apart – could have imagined.

3 Lives of Quiet Desperation

Burt Lancaster began the 1950s with the first of only two truly swashbuckling yarns he was to make in his career. It is a measure of the impact he made in these two films that for many years the public was inclined to associate him with such tales. Similarly affected were the minds of several critics who should have known better, if only because they were being paid to be smarter than the rest of the moviegoing public.

Surprising though it might be, Hollywood, never noted for failing to do the obvious, didn't pick up on Lancaster's acrobatic skills right from the start. Instead, it was left to Lancaster himself briefly to exploit his special athletic talents.

Following his first four highly encouraging years in pictures, Lancaster's business relationship with Harold Hecht took a firm grip on the actor's career. The quality of his early films had given no grounds for serious complaint, but he was well aware of the ever-present threat of typecasting. The success of his 1940s *films noirs* almost put him in a rut. Had this happened his future might well have been bleak, because the *noir* category dwindled during the 1950s and all but expired by the end of that decade.

Control of his career allowed Lancaster to direct his fast-developing acting ability into westerns, adventure stories, straight dramatic roles and, almost in passing, a couple of the swash and buckle tales for which his acrobatic athleticism was so well suited.

The Flame and the Arrow (1950) gave full rein to this athletic prowess, but it is more than just another adventure movie. The story line, while outwardly a transposed version of the Robin Hood/William Tell stories (indeed, it was shot on the leftover sets of an earlier Robin Hood film), contains elements of a worthy social conscience encouraging opposition to tyranny. The crisp screenplay by Waldo Salt (his last full credit before his 1951 blacklisting) is subtly realized by Jacques Tourneur's direction, which never lets the message obstruct the derring-do. As a result of this combination of action and (admittedly simplistic) philosophy, *The Flame and the Arrow*, despite its deliberate comic-book overlay, is one of the few films in its genre which stands up to repeated viewings.

The story line is essentially story-book simple: Dardo Bartoli, known as the Arrow (Lancaster), takes Princess Anne (Virginia Mayo) as his prisoner, using her as hostage for the release of his son, Rudy (Gordon Gerbert), held captive by Anne's uncle, Ulrich of Hesse, known as the Hawk (Frank Allenby), who has also taken under his evil wing Dardo's estranged wife, Francesca (Lynn Baggett).

Dardo sends a written demand to Ulrich but the messenger, the mute Piccolo (Nick Cravat), is flogged. Worse, Ulrich prepares to hang Dardo's uncle and threatens to execute several local villagers unless the outlaw surrenders. Dardo agrees, having first devised an elaborate scheme which involves a fake hanging. With Dardo's men imprisoned in the castle dungeons and Dardo's supposedly dead body carried from the gallows by the mourning villagers, Ulrich and his men celebrate.

Dardo and Piccolo enter the castle disguised as mummers and join in the entertainment. 'I always knew we should've been acrobats,' Dardo says to his partner in a far from in-joke.

Releasing his comrades from the dungeons, Dardo eventually overcomes Ulrich's men only to find that his enemy has murdered Francesca. He dispatches the villain with an arrow through the heart, indulges in an exultant display of acrobatics before being happily reunited with his son and Princess Anne.

The bare bones are clearly those of a thousand skeletal Hollywood costume dramas, but *The Flame and the Arrow* exceeds expectations by a considerable margin. The historical setting, twelfth-century Lombardy under the grip of Frederick Barbarossa, is Hollywood-vague but a timeless and universal message about tyranny and populism somehow comes through all the high jinks.

Main credit for the film's quality and its unstoppable vitality lies with the director. A disciple of Val Lewton, Tourneur directed several of the master's classic horror films at RKO. These included *I Walked with a Zombie, The Leopard Man* (both 1943) and the extraordinary *Cat People* (1942). Although he worked in many genres and in various countries, including Britain, Tourneur's real gifts lay in the restrained, suspenseful field of the low-budget horror flick (although, because of the manner in which he evoked his desired effect from audiences, the word 'terror' might be substituted for 'horror'). Far removed as it is from such genres, *The Flame and the Arrow* benefits throughout its exhilarating footage from its director's professionalism and craftsmanship.

Lancaster ran away with the acting honours, his zest and enthusiasm more than compensating for an only average supporting cast headed by Virginia Mayo's customary painted-doll performance. Moreover, he is clearly relishing the opportunity to act *and* perform impressive acrobatic feats on screen. The undercurrent of liberal idealism which was to illuminate many later Lancaster roles makes one of its earliest appearances here but, understandably enough given the setting, it is the athleticism that sticks in the mind.

Among the activities surrounding publicity for the film was a tour undertaken by Lancaster and Cravat in which they worked at their old routines with Cole Brothers Circus; but going back in time was not as much fun as they thought it would be – even if they were being paid $11,000 a week. Also heavily publicized was the fact that Lancaster had done all the movie acrobatics himself; and Warner Brothers offered a million dollars to anyone who could prove otherwise. A stunt double and bit-part player named Jules Garrison thought he could so prove and had to take his claim to court before he discovered that Warners' lawyers were too smart to have left open any loopholes. As it happens, apart from two or three long shots taken when Lancaster was busy elsewhere, it really is the star who does all the impressive feats.

Neither legal hassles nor acrobatics affected Lancaster's next film which was something hitherto untried in his career.

In *Mr 880* (1950) Steve Buchanan (Lancaster) is a US Treasury investigator on the trail of an inept counterfeiter who has evaded capture for years by dint of churning out only a few one dollar bills and spreading them far and wide. The counterfeiter uses the same plate with the same serial number (hence the name by which the T-men know him). Steve draws close to his quarry through a bill unwittingly passed by Ann Winslow (Dorothy McGuire), who lives in the same building as the counterfeiter, 'Skipper' Miller (Edmund Gwenn), a determinedly dear little old man.

Mr 880 continues· to evade capture, mainly because Steve loses his concentration when he becomes romantically involved with Ann. In the end Mr 880 is collared but a kindly judge lets him off with the mildest of sentences.

Written by Robert Riskin from an apparently genuine case (the counterfeiter, not the romantic T-man), the morality is reminiscent of some of the writer's work with Frank Capra. The 'little man' prevails against the might of the state and what does it matter if a few laws are broken so long as nobody is really hurt. It is a simplistic, almost simple-minded, philosophy which few of today's audiences can stomach, and although played as whimsical comedy, the film now has a very dated air.

Fans equating T-man with G-man and expecting rough stuff and gunplay were disappointed, and the film did poor business. Whether or not this was a factor in deciding his future career philosophy, it was to be more than three decades before Lancaster again tried his hand at light comedy.

Action fans disappointed by *Mr 880* crowded back for Lancaster's next film, his first western. In the event, *Vengeance Valley* (1951), while having a fair helping of tough, two-fisted action, is rather more thoughtful than most horse operas of its time.

Old Arch Strobie (Ray Collins), a rancher, has two sons, one natural the other adopted. The natural son, Lee (Robert Walker), is a scoundrel while Owen (Lancaster) works hard and conscientiously for his adopted father. When Lee, who is married to Jen (Joanne Dru), gets another girl, Lily (Sally Forrest), pregnant Owen contrives to keep the news from Arch. Owen's actions mislead Lily's vengeful brothers, doing him no good at all, as they believe him to be responsible for their sister's plight. Neither does this help Owen in his hoped-for relationship with Jen, but when Lee tricks his father out of a share of the ranch and makes off with the livestock Owen reckons the time has come for a man to do what a man's gotta do. After steering the wayward cattle back home he kills Lee in a gunfight, then rides home to the new widow's welcoming arms.

Encouragingly long on character development, the film tries hard not to be a run-of-the-mill western but lacks the panache needed to make the grade. Everyone performs well, with Lancaster and Walker, an unusually cultivated actor to be found in western garb, giving interestingly contrasted interpretations of standard western roles.

Already, Lancaster's choice of roles in the 1950s was proving rich in variety and the range was extended still further when he played the eponymous real-life hero in *Jim Thorpe, All-American* (1951).

Jim Thorpe was an American Indian (his given name was Bright Path) who became one of his country's foremost athletes. In the 1912 Stockholm Olympic Games Thorpe was a double gold medallist, winning both the pentathlon and the decathlon before it was revealed that two years earlier he had played professional baseball. His amateur status thus impugned, his Olympic honours were stripped from him and he fell from grace.

In 1931, while working as a construction-site labourer, Thorpe was hired by a fellow Indian, actor-agent Iron Eyes Cody, and began working as an extra in the movies. At the 1932 Los Angeles Olympics Thorpe was applauded enthusiastically by the crowd when he turned up as a spectator. Quite clearly, earlier public outrage at his 'crime' of earning money from sport had been forgotten.

By the 1950s Thorpe was fully restored to favour and was acclaimed by American sports writers as their country's greatest twentieth-century athlete.

Inevitably, Hollywood took an interest, Warner Brothers having already bought the rights to Thorpe's autobiography, and, when it was realized that in Burt Lancaster they had an actor who was physically suited to the part, a bio-pic was put into production.

It was equally inevitable that the film-makers could not resist embellishing a story already filled with enough dramatic detail to enhance half a dozen films. The result was a sentimentalized version of Thorpe's life, something completely inappropriate for a man with his gritty determination. (They also 'cleaned up' his image a little, apparently believing that three marriages and six kids was unsuitable – the script gave him one wife and one child.)

Lancaster's portrayal of the 'Man of Bronze' was effective enough given the limitations of the screenplay (he had been partly attracted by the implications of racism in the hounding Thorpe received, but this element was well watered down). The combination of his physical power and grace and his restrained acting fits well with the true nature of the ill-fated athlete.

Jim Thorpe died in 1953 and in 1982 his name was returned to the record books and his medals restored to his family. At the Los Angeles Olympic Games of 1984, an occasion where brash commercialism made nonsense of the reason for Thorpe's disgrace, the gaudy opening ceremony contained at least one moment of honesty as Jim Thorpe's grandson entered the arena as a standard-bearer.

From a well-meaning but failed attempt to recapture the life of a real man, Lancaster's next film was an easily forgettable Foreign Legion spoof. *Ten Tall Men* (1951) had no pretensions and was played largely for rough and ready laughs. Among the mob of legionnaires supporting Lancaster's Sergeant Mike Kincaid were Irish actor Keiron Moore and one of Hollywood's most endearing stock Latins, the splendidly hammy Gilbert Roland.

A pattern was starting to emerge in Lancaster's work. He appeared regularly in films with reasonably assured box-office success, regardless of what he might have thought of them. This gave him financial breathing-space which allowed him, whenever he could, to work in films which had – or at least tried to have – something to say. The money also helped finance productions of films he and Harold Hecht wanted to make, but which had no role for him as an actor. An example of this is *The First Time* (1952), a light, fast-paced comedy directed by Frank Tashlin and starring Robert Cummings and Barbara Hale.

Domestically, Lancaster was becoming even more settled; and his family home became ever more crowded with the arrival, in 1952, of a second daughter whom he and Norma named Joanna.

With his next film, his second and last outright swashbuckler, Lancaster paid homage to Douglas Fairbanks, the film actor he had admired during his childhood visits to the nickelodean. *The*

Crimson Pirate (1952) was made in Europe (interiors shot at Teddington, England; location shooting on the island of Ischia in the Mediterranean) and proved to be a magnificent romp, tossing in every known pirate-movie cliché on its way to becoming a spoof of the whole genre.

To work, a spoof has to have integrity and its own high standards of production, and *The Crimson Pirate* had these qualities in abundance.

The film reunited the star with director Robert Siodmak, but this differed greatly from their previous collaborations. From the opening moments the audience is left in no doubt that the dark seriousness of *The Killers* and *Criss Cross* is not to be repeated. Even the underlying serious purpose of Lancaster's other swashbuckler, *The Flame and the Arrow*, was not a part of this venture into the territory Fairbanks and Errol Flynn had made their own. This is a fun picture which never lets up from its opening moments, as Captain Vallo (Lancaster) swings athletically up into the rigging of his pirate ship and addresses the camera:

'Gather round, lads and lasses, gather round. You've been shanghai'd aboard for the last cruise of the Crimson Pirate. A long, long time ago in the far, far Caribbean. Remember, in a pirate ship, in pirate waters, in a pirate world. Ask no questions, believe only what you see. No! Believe only half of what you see.'

With tongue firmly in cheek, the film follows the fortunes of the redoubtable Cap'n Vallo and his faithful (and some not-so-faithful) pirate crew. Among the faithful are Prudence (James Hayter) and Ojo (Nick Cravat). This was the best of Cravat's roles with his old tumbling-act partner. Here he again appears as a mute (the most effective way of concealing his East Side New York accent). The comic aspirations of *The Crimson Pirate* are well realized in a scene where Vallo, Prudence and Ojo, dressed as women, dance together. Lancaster in drag might seem an unlikely image, but the scene works beautifully because there is none of the self-consciousness that causes most he-man actors to over-assert their masculinity on such occasions. In Pauline Kael's words, Lancaster is a scrambled cartoon of a woman.

Vallo's antics generate some tension among his crew

members, who plot his downfall. Among the unfaithful is Humble Bellows (Torin Thatcher), who has one of the film's better lines when he complains to his captain, 'We can't leave a pretty woman unmolested on board ship. It'll give piracy a bad name.'

Any doubts about screenwriter Roland Kibbee's cheerfully irreverent approach to his task can be determined from one of Vallo's exhortations to his men:

'Pack on all canvas, you hairy-tailed sea snakes.'

A quick flash of the famous Lancaster teeth, then:

'Go get 'em.'

Homage to Douglas Fairbanks took concrete form in a scene in which Lancaster, high in the rigging, drives his sword through a sail then slides down to the deck, slitting the sail as he goes. Fairbanks had done the same spectacular stunt in *The Black Pirate* (1920). Such a good stunt (achieved by fixing a rigid blade through the sail and running the whole thing down a length of piano wire hidden at the back of the sail) was too good to use only once or twice and another swashbuckler, *Against All Flags* (1952), starring Errol Flynn, also used it.

The film critic of the *New York Times*, signing his review A.W., not only enjoyed the film but liked the star too. 'Burt Lancaster is truly a picture pirate. A blond, smiling, muscular and agile athlete he leads the climactic fight ... with the bounce and élan of a tumbler at an opening night under the Big Top.' With Bosley Crowther presumably safely out of range, A.W. was even moved to applaud Lancaster's old mate from his days as an acrobat. 'As his mute lieutenant, Nick Cravat needs no lines to add enough comic pantomimic bits to earn his share of the laughs.'

However, Cravat's performance did not keep him safe from his erstwhile partner's tongue when things did not go as well as he thought they should.

By now, Lancaster's habit of castigating fellow performers was well known; he had already begun arguing with directors. On *Brute Force* he had directed director Jules Dassin; while working on *Desert Fury* he had told Hal Wallis that he would soon be ready to direct his own films. On *Crimson Pirate* he clashed angrily with Robert Siodmak, occasionally upbraiding him savagely in front of the cast and crew.

For all such outbursts of anger, the finished product is an action-packed fun film and it holds up well today, when very different kinds of action are what most filmgoers seek. For all that it remains his solitary venture into the genre, *The Crimson Pirate* places Burt Lancaster at the shoulder of his childhood screen idol, Douglas Fairbanks. Indeed, even the redoubtable Errol Flynn is edged a little to one side, if only because Lancaster displays more tongue-in-cheek enjoyment in his spectacular feats.

With Lancaster's next film there was, once again, a marked contrast. From the fun and frolics of colourful piracy, he took the role of the depressed, struggling, alcoholic Doc Delaney in *Come Back, Little Sheba* (1952).

Delaney is the husband of the slatternly Lola (Shirley Booth, who had played the role on Broadway), a pathetically well-meaning woman who both gives and craves affection indiscriminately. Lola is unable to perceive that her cloying love is overwhelming and destroying her weak husband.

Lodging with the Delaneys is Marie Buckholder (Terry Moore), a young girl whose own emotional life is tangled and uncertain. Marie seeks Lola's advice and Doc, aware that his wife is directing the girl into the kind of hopelessly romantic never-never land she herself inhabits, turns increasingly to drink.

For the first time, Lola is compelled to see the life of quiet desperation her husband has been leading. She is forced into making a choice. If she continues in her ways she will destroy Doc; if she accepts reality and forces herself to change there is at least a chance that they will salvage something from the unhappiness of their life together.

The screenplay by Ketti Frings was based upon William Inge's stage play while the direction came from Daniel Mann, who had also directed the Broadway version. *Come Back, Little Sheba* was Mann's first screen credit and it had also been his Broadway début, thereby giving him an unusual double (his later Broadway credits included *The Rose Tattoo* and *Paint Your Wagon*).

There is a measure of staginess in the screen version of *Come Back, Little Sheba* but this mostly suits the overpowering atmosphere Lola generates in the Delaney household.

Lancaster necessarily takes second place to his co-star, but his performance is full of insight and he is wholly supportive to her demanding role. Much younger than the character he portrays, he manages to convey the man's surface humility which is underscored by the towering frustration of the man Doc Delaney once had been. Indeed, few actors of Lancaster's age and stature would have given such unstinting support to a co-star, and the manner in which he conducted himself on and off the set indicates exceptional professional maturity.

At one point, from being critical of his co-workers' efforts, he found himself on the receiving end of criticism when Shirley Booth constructively remarked, 'Burt, once in a while you hit a note of truth and you can hear a bell ring, but most of the time I can see the wheels turning and your brain working.'

Lancaster's apparent unsuitability for the role of Doc caused some problems at the time when the film was in pre-production, and years later memories had clouded who persuaded whom. In a 1973 interview with Gordon Gow, Lancaster indicated that he had wanted the role and had to pressurize Hal Wallis to be allowed to tackle it. Twenty years earlier, interviewed by William H. Brownell Jr for the *New York Times*, Lancaster had suggested that the reluctance was his, and only the encouragement of Michael Curtiz, who had directed him in *Jim Thorpe, All-American*, swung both himself and Wallis towards the idea. In this same 1950s interview Lancaster observed that his role as Doc provided 'the best opportunity to act I've ever had'. He was very enthusiastic about his co-star. Shirley Booth was 'an inspiration … she worked so hard to adapt the part to the motion-picture screen, which is anything but easy when you've grown to play a character in a certain way over months of constant association'.

Reviewers of the day were generally complimentary, especially about Shirley Booth who deservedly won an Oscar as Best Actress for her portrayal of Lola Delaney. As time passed, however, Lancaster's significance in his role became more apparent. Lionel Godfrey, writing in *Films and Filming* in October 1966 commented: 'Lancaster's gentle utterance of Doc's repeated line – "Dreams are funny" – memorably captures the character's sadness and wistful longing, and for those who specialize in surprisedly "discovering" his great ability, here is one of a long string of opportunities provided by this fine actor.'

In the March 1962 issue of *Films and Filming* John Howard Reid had recalled Henry David Thoreau's phrase, 'the mass of men lead lives of quiet desperation', which admirably suits not only Doc Delaney but many other characters Lancaster chose to portray throughout his career. Reid rightly saw this as the theme of the film, and then went on to say of Lancaster that he is 'an excellent, even a brilliant actor; indeed, I would go so far as to affirm that he is the finest player in the United States today'. Praise indeed; and largely warranted, although anyone reading such fulsome remarks prior to seeing Lancaster's next film would be justified in wondering what all the fuss was about.

South Sea Woman (1953) fulfilled Lancaster's contractual obligations with Warners and that is about the only positive thing that can be said about it.

Set in the Pacific during World War II, the story charts the adventures of a couple of marines and a singer (Lancaster, Chuck Connors and Virginia Mayo) who sink a floating nightclub and a Japanese destroyer with equal casualness and, apparently, loss of life.

Pausing only for a swift guest spot in *Three Sailors and a Girl* (1953), a musical with songs by Sammy Fain and Sammy Cahn, Lancaster moved on to a role which kept him in uniform and in the Pacific Ocean but all resemblance to his previous starring role ended there.

Based upon James Jones's powerful novel of the same name, *From Here to Eternity* (1953) was one of a growing number of Hollywood films of the 1950s which ignored the prevailing gung-ho approach to war.

Set (and filmed) at Schofield Barracks, Hawaii, the story examines the lives of two mismatched couples living there in 1941. One couple is Private Robert E. Lee Prewitt (Montgomery Clift) and Alma Burke (Donna Reed), who begin a love affair when he visits the New Congress Club, where she provides female companionship for the troops. (In the movie, the club is apparently a social club which veils its origins in the novel where it is unmistakably a brothel.) The other couple is Sergeant Milt Warden (Lancaster) and Karen Holmes (Deborah Kerr), the wife of his immediate superior, Captain Dana Holmes (Philip Ober). When Warden falls in love with Karen he endangers his career and his freedom because the penalty for committing adultery with an officer's wife is twenty years in military prison.

Prewitt, only recently arrived at Schofield, is an able fighter and Captain Holmes, who handles the company's boxing squad is eager to recruit him. Holmes, a career officer, believes that success in sports is one of few ways up the ladder of promotion in peacetime and is bitterly angry when Prewitt refuses to fight. Unaware that Prewitt's last fight ended in tragedy when his opponent was blinded, Holmes encourages the rest of the boxing squad to pressurize the reluctant fighter.

Meanwhile, Karen Holmes, neglected by her husband, is ripe for an affair and responds to Warden's advances.

Although outwardly dissimilar, Prewitt and Warden have some things in common. Both are devoted to the army, despite their awareness of its potential for corrupting men who are unsuited to the power they hold over men's lives. Each man also decides that the way to win the woman he loves is to advance his career.

If Prewitt rises in the ranks he will be acceptable to the snobbish, materialistic Alma; if Warden becomes an officer he will be able to marry Karen after she is divorced.

But other events overtake these private decisions. Prewitt's closest friend, Maggio (Frank Sinatra), dies from a beating administered while he is in the stockade. Prewitt avenges his friend's death by killing the brutish Fatso (Ernest Borgnine), then hides out with Alma.

When Holmes is dismissed from the service for the manner in which he has behaved towards the men in his command, the way is clear for Warden and Karen, but for a while he still seeks promotion. Eventually, he changes his mind and Karen uses this as an excuse to talk herself out of their affair.

Then the Japanese take a hand in events and attack Pearl Harbor. Prewitt decides to return to barracks and Alma, by his decision forced to face reality, abandons her illusory world (she calls herself 'Lorene', a more glamorous name) and tells him she will take him as he is. But it is too late for that: Prewitt is going back to a court-martial. But even this fateful decision is taken out of his hands. As he approaches the barracks a guard, unnerved by the sudden state of war, shoots him dead.

Milt Warden speaks the eulogy over Prewitt's coffin, declaring that if Prewitt had been the kind of man the army wanted him to be he would be alive. Because he was guilty of being independent of mind and spirit, he died. By implication, Warden is also talking about himself.

For all its generally high quality there are some awkward moments in the film's structure. Among these is Warden's erratic behaviour at the point in the film where he no longer needs to become an officer but persists for a while in his attempt; this may be a hangover from changes made in transferring the novel to the screen. Originally, Holmes was not dismissed (the film action which clears the way for Warden and Karen) but promoted. In the 1950s Hollywood would have thought that too cynical. Similarly affected by contemporary attitudes is the contrast between Holmes and Prewitt in the moral stance they take on violence. Prewitt, tough-minded and physically capable, is peaceful and determined not to be sucked into mindless militancy; Holmes epitomizes the unseemly face of military might, so concerned with personal advancement that he is blind to signs of imminent war. This, too, was not generally the stuff of which 1950s war movies were made.

The performances of the four principals, and in all the main supporting roles, are of a very high standard and the film gained ten nominations for Academy Awards of which six, including Frank Sinatra and Donna Reed as Best Supporting Actor and Actress, were successful.

Among the unsuccessful nominees were Lancaster and Montgomery Clift. In retrospect, the least well served by the decision of those who sat on the judging committee was Clift. His interpretation of the quietly stubborn, gentle-natured Prewitt was one of the best of his many fine screen performances. He also was the first, and possibly the last, actor to unnerve Lancaster, who afterwards confessed to approaching his scenes with Clift with his knees literally trembling.

Perhaps the best-remembered scene in *From Here to Eternity* is that in which Lancaster and Deborah Kerr make love on a wave-lapped beach. One of the hottest things of its time, today it seems mild and almost chaste in its old-fashioned discretion. Yet the scene does have power, especially when viewed as whole. Usually, when it is screened independently of the film, the scene stops after the passionate embrace in the waves. Yet what happens next, as Warden angrily denounces Karen for the very thing that attracted him to her in the first place – her sexuality – is a powerful dramatic statement. Like many men in his position, he cannot accept the fact that the woman with whom he is having an affair has previously had affairs with other men.

Lancaster's portrayal of Milt Warden is a fine one with all the undertones of a complex character carefully delineated. Despite his fear of Montgomery Clift, he dominates his scenes by his physical presence, but never lets this unbalance the prevailing mood. Whether confronting the vicious Fatso (softly urging, 'Come on, come on,' as the other man circles him with a knife), responding romantically to Karen, or drunkenly commiserating with Prewitt, he provides a solid and reliable core to the entire film.

Although the Best Actor Oscar eluded him on this occasion (it went to William Holden for *Stalag 17*), his career was at an artistic and commercial high point. *From Here to Eternity*, perhaps more than any other of his previous films, combined all the elements of success: artistic merit, box-office appeal, critical and public acclaim.

He also managed to avoid alienating such powerful individuals as Hollywood gossip columnist Hedda Hopper, even though, running against the trend followed by the majority of his fellow actors, he refused to kowtow to her. In an interview with Hopper, whom he addressed by her surname, he told her that he didn't frighten easily and that she didn't scare him at all. He also remarked that her manner reminded him of his mother. The columnist assumed that this was a compliment, when it was clear that he had meant it as anything but that.

After less than a decade in the motion-picture business, Lancaster was able to review with satisfaction the position he had attained. Although the 1950s were not yet half-way through, he and Harold Hecht used his successes, culminating in the international acclaim accorded to *From Here to Eternity*, by beginning to develop their production company often with scant regard for commercial considerations. The pattern which thus emerged, of using box-office success in one film to help finance another which has only artistic merit on its side, was one which was to remain a Lancaster trait for the rest of his career.

Lancaster also began testing himself even more as an actor,

seeking out roles which placed demands upon him regardless of whether or not they had box-office appeal. The reason for this is simple: what had started out almost as an accidental career (and one he had even, as a child, tried to avoid) had become something very different. He had discovered inside himself another passion to place alongside those for books, paintings and music. This was a passion for acting.

4 Silent and Deep

In 1954, Burt Lancaster and Harold Hecht changed the name of their production company from Hecht–Norma to Hecht–Lancaster.

Their motivation was in part to have the obvious advantage of using the weight of Lancaster's name where everyone could see it. Additionally, the company's current distribution arrangement was with Warner Brothers and this was about to expire and be replaced by a deal with United Artists.

The last Hecht–Norma/Warner Brothers film was *His Majesty O'Keefe* (1954), a semi-swashbuckler set in the Pacific and filmed on the island of Viti Levu, the largest of the Fiji Islands.

Warners had British currency tied up and this was a way of unfreezing funds. The company also benefited from the parsimony of the British Colonial Government which, in its anxiety to preserve the status quo, insisted that natives employed as extras should not receive more than a dollar a day for their services.

The main setting for the film was on Deuba Beach, about thirty-five miles from the capital, Suva. Part of the film company's contract with the government was that after they were finished they would leave behind their specially constructed village as a means of helping to alleviate a local housing shortage.

For all the financial attractions of filming on Fiji, the production unit soon learned that these were considerably outweighed by the adversities of the climate, and the islands never took off as a favoured film location. The star certainly had no wish ever to work there again, commenting to an interviewer that 'it was so tough working in the humidity that one day I actually watched fungus grow on my clothes'.

For all the problems imposed by the climate, there was a holiday atmosphere about the location, as Lancaster had decided to take Norma and the children with him on the trip. The romantic tropical setting may have wrought its own kind of influence, because later that year Norma gave birth to their third daughter, whom they named Sighle (pronounced Sheila).

As for the film, despite the lush tropical setting it proved to be rather ordinary. Directed by Byron Haskin and with the experienced Borden Chase collaborating on the screenplay, it was flat and laborious where it should have been high-spirited and fast-moving.

Lancaster next made a trio of westerns, each very different from the others and with equally dissimilar roles for him.

First of these was *Apache* (1954), one of several films of the period which looked sympathetically, and in a spirit of reconciliation, at the manner in which Native Americans had been treated by the invading white man.

The story of *Apache* had its roots in historical fact. When the majority of the Apaches under the leadership of Geronimo surrendered to the white man in the 1880s, some of their number refused to be subjugated and began a series of small wars against the invaders. In some cases, small groups fought guerrilla actions; in a few instances, individuals took up arms against the might of the state. Occasionally, as depicted in *Apache*, a Native American sought not merely to kill, but to try to live in peace on the land he thought of as his home.

The ability of the Apache to live off the inhospitable desert lands in the south-western states proved far superior to that of the better equipped and numerically overwhelming forces of the US Cavalry. Pursuit of so-called renegades often lasted for years.

In *Apache*, a lone warrior named Massai (Lancaster) and his wife Nalinle (Jean Peters) try to come to terms with the changing face of the land over which they could once roam freely. At first Massai tries force; killing and risking being killed in defence of his freedom. Later, with his wife pregnant with their first child, Massai attempts to settle down.

Eventually. Massai is trapped by pursuing white men in the middle of the pathetic little field of corn planted with seed garnered by Nalinle. With no possible means of escape, he prepares to fight what must be his last battle. Then he hears the cry of his new-born baby, and the leader of his persecutors, Al Sieber (John McIntire), calls off his men.

This ending was a last-minute change; in the screenplay (based upon Paul I. Wellman's book *Bronco Apache*) Massai was shot in the back as he turned towards his child. The distributors felt that this was an ending Lancaster's fans would dislike, and persuaded him to make the change. Given the fact that the real-life Al Sieber was almost pathological in his hatred of Native Americans, the new ending missed reality by a substantial margin.

Not surprisingly perhaps, considering that Hollywood helped perpetuate the myth of heroism surrounding such crazed killers as Jesse James, Billy the Kid and Al Capone, Al Sieber turned up in films in a number of guises over the years: Charlton Heston played him in *Arrowhead* (1953) while John Wayne's Ethan Edwards in *The Searchers* (1956) is the best known representation of this dubious hero.

Very low-key, *Apache* benefits from sound performances from the two principals. Lancaster makes his character sympathetic, while never undermining his strength; Jean Peters vividly portrays a wife who struggles to establish her own identity in the face of her husband's apparent indifference.

For all the success of their on-screen partnership, off-screen the two stars were constantly at odds with one another. Simultaneously, Peters was having contractual problems with Twentieth Century-Fox. She made only two more films before ending a brief career in 1955. Two years later she married billionaire recluse Howard Hughes whom she divorced in 1971. In 1973 she returned to acting, this time on television.

The director of *Apache* was Robert Aldrich, working on his first big-budget film. He and Lancaster were together on the star's next film and this time it was they who didn't get along.

Vera Cruz (1954) uses the reliable central theme of two tough-minded loners who form a temporary and strained partnership, based upon mutual mistrust and cautious admiration. One is an out-and-out good guy Benjamin Trane (Gary Cooper), the other is a good-bad guy Joe Erin (Lancaster). In case anyone was in any doubt about their personal characteristics, Lancaster was dressed in black with silver trimmings (a costume he selected himself), while Cooper appeared to be wearing the same clothes he'd worn in his last dozen westerns.

Down-at-heel and dusty though he might be, Cooper shines with honesty and integrity in this tale of two mercenaries in Mexico during the war between the forces of rebel leader Benito Juarez and Emperor Maximilian. When Trane and Erin eventually get their hands on the gold (there's always gold in movies set in Mexico), the good guy decides it is time to listen to his conscience and hand it over to the rebels. Needless to say, the bad guy fails to agree with this plan; he wants the gold for himself. The two men shoot it out and, this being the way things were in 1950s Hollywood, good triumphs over evil.

The scenes between Cooper and Lancaster are all good and there is no sign of the disagreements which Iron Eyes Cody reports in his autobiography. Not content with arguing with director Robert Aldrich, it seems that Lancaster also castigated the highly experienced Cooper over his acting technique.

A strong supporting cast includes George Macready, Cesar Romero, Charles Bronson (who was also in *Apache*) and Ernest Borgnine.

A frequently violent film, *Vera Cruz* met with critical indifference with Bosley Crowther remarking in the *New York Times* that Lancaster 'indeed is a mess as a villain who displays his meanness by frequent diabolic laughs'. The fans loved it.

During the mid-1950s, Lancaster and Hecht employed James Hill as story editor. He was Borden Chase's co-writer on *His Majesty O'Keefe* and had produced *Vera Cruz*. Hill's involvement with the company grew and he became steadily more important to their successes (becoming a full partner towards the end of the decade). In 1955, all three men were instrumental in bringing to the screen a remarkable film which broke many of Hollywood's self-imposed rules about what would and would not succeed at the box office.

Marty (1955) was based upon a television play by Paddy Chayefsky and told the story of a man and woman, both unattractive by conventional standards, both leading dull lives, both doomed to solitary unhappiness. Against all the odds, these two people find happiness in one another.

And it was against all the odds that *Marty* won four Oscars: Ernest Borgnine as Best Actor, Delbert Mann as Best Director,

Paddy Chayefsky for his screenplay, and Best Picture. The film also made money; $5.5 million against production costs of one-third of a million.

For all this, *Marty* trailed problems after it, with Ernest Borgnine suing Lancaster's production company for money he claimed he was owed under the terms of his contract. He also levelled charges that the terms and conditions of his contract were such that they inhibited the development of his career. The legal hassles dragged on for a couple of years before being settled to the plaintiff's satisfaction.

In the mean time, Lancaster's third western in a row had had its share of problems.

Several years had passed since Lancaster had stated his intention of directing his own films. While he certainly did not lack the confidence, some might say the arrogance, needed to undertake this task, his expertise was soon in question as work on *The Kentuckian* (1955) began. Worst of all, some of his earlier outbursts against the directors for whom he had worked came back to haunt him.

When he filed his application for membership of the Screen Directors Guild it was denied because he had 'publicly expressed opinions of contempt for our members in the newspapers and over TV'.

However, the Guild granted a waiver to allow him to make the film, indicating that when it was completed he could reapply. While the Guild doubtless had an eye on the fact that refusal might affect the livelihoods of the many people involved in the making of a film, they were probably also hoping that the experience would teach Lancaster that a director's lot was not an especially happy one.

The Kentuckian is a simple-minded adventure yarn set in the early nineteenth century (a period with which Hollywood has never really come to terms). The tale follows attempts by Eli Wakefield (Lancaster) and his young son, Little Eli (Donald MacDonald), to journey to Texas where they plan to start a new life. They take with them Hannah (Dianne Foster), a serving-girl whose indentures Eli buys with his savings after she helps Eli escape the attentions of his enemies.

Lightly handled, with touches of romance, a few songs and a modicum of tough stuff (including a fight between bare-fisted

Lancaster and bullwhip-wielding Walter Matthau in his first screen role), the film is undemanding of its audience. At the time of its release, it was quite refreshing to see an adventure story told in this relaxed and light-hearted manner. Seen today, it appears slow and rather aimless, but is perhaps best summed up by Lancaster himself who with hindsight called it 'a very pleasant little film'.

The Kentuckian did, however, place a considerable amount of pressure upon Lancaster in his multiple roles of star, director and co-producer. In retrospect, he conceded that he had taken on too much; telling Gordon Gow in *Hollywood in the Fifties*, that trying to act and direct was a mistake he would not repeat. 'If and when I direct another film, I will not act in it', he declared.

It appeared as though the Directors Guild's thinking was vindicated.

For his next film role, Lancaster was reunited with producer Hal Wallis and, as had happened on past collaborations, he had to pitch hard before he was allowed to play a part which appeared unsuitable for him.

The Rose Tattoo (1955) was based by Tennessee Williams upon his own stage play. Much of the story's hot and steamy sensuality stems from Williams's concept of life in the Deep South and, however effective this might be on the stage, on screen it often appears too stylized.

Here, Serafina Delle Rose (Anna Magnani) longs for and still lusts after her dead husband, a lover of legendary prowess. When slow-witted truck driver Alvaro Mangiacavallo (Lancaster) is stranded in town, his physical resemblance to the dead man – even to the tattooed rose both men bore – allied to his animal sexuality, encourages Serafina to exploit him, as she attempts to fill the void left in her life by her husband's death.

Serafina's daughter Rosa (Marisa Pavan) wants to marry Jack Hunter (Ben Johnson), a simple sailor, but Serafina objects to their relationship. However, her resistance to the young lovers and her rejection of the world in general, and of men in particular, are swept aside when Alvaro reawakens her sexuality.

The implications of the tale are highly sexist; all Serafina needs to snap her out of her decline is the appearance in her life of a sexual athlete. The tragedy of the story is that not even the redoubtable Alvaro can really replace the dead man. Indeed, not even Serafina's husband could really measure up to the heights imagined for him by his widow. The legend is a product of her mind; in reality, her husband was deceitful and two-timing.

For all the power of the writing, the plot stands on shaky foundations, but the structure doesn't topple, thanks almost entirely to Magnani's dominating central performance which is everything that a Tennessee Williams heroine should be.

Lancaster's support is effective, and the film was well directed by Daniel Mann and strikingly photographed by James Wong Howe.

The Rose Tattoo did well at the Academy Awards with Oscars going to writer, cinematographer and to Anna Magnani as Best Actress. With the concurrent successes of *Marty*, this was substantial recognition for Lancaster's involvement in the motion-picture industry. It was also the second time that his insistence upon playing supporting roles to powerful women resulted in the award of a Best Actress Oscar.

From the strange ground of Tennessee Williams's Deep South, Lancaster next moved into familiar territory when, for the first time, he made a film about the circus.

Trapeze (1956) follows the fortunes of a young aerialist, Tino Orsini (Tony Curtis), whose ambition is to perform the difficult triple somersault. He seeks the help of veteran Mike Ribble (Lancaster), now crippled after a fall but still the best catcher in the business.

When their double act at the Paris-based Circus Bouglione is invaded by the glamorous Lola (Gina Lollobrigida) problems ensue. Tino falls for Lola, but Mike, who also secretly loves her, insists she will ruin the act. When the two men come to blows, Mike realizes that this is a recipe for disaster and leaves the act. But when an American impresario visits the circus Mike knows that this is Tino's big chance, and he returns to help him achieve his triple leap.

With the young flyer on his way to a great future, Mike decides to quit the circus and Lola chooses to go with him.

Both plot and character development leave rather a lot to be desired and the screenplay, which was based upon a novel by Max Catto, is largely at fault. (A writer named Daniel Fuchs had other ideas about the film's origins and, believing it to be based upon his short story *The Daring Young Man*, published in *Colliers*, sued for more than $8 million.)

The film was a popular success with generally good reviews. *Variety* called it 'high-flying screen entertainment equipped with everything necessary to attract' while John Wilcox, writing in *Sight & Sound*, commented that Lancaster 'plays sympathetically as Mike and always conveys the sense of being emotionally involved in the story'.

Wilcox also drew attention to the apparently impossible fact that, despite her tights and spangled slippers, unflattering camera angles made La Lollo look ungainly.

Undoubtedly, this film brought back memories for the star who had long wanted to make a film about the circus. (For some of the highly specialized work needed in this film, Lancaster used a double; the man chosen was Eddie Ward whom he knew from his own circus days back in the 1930s.)

Although at the time few were aware of it, Lancaster's private life was currently developing a measure of instability. Despite the closeness of his relationship with his wife, Lancaster clearly had an eye for the ladies. In an interview he had once remarked, light-heartedly but apparently not entirely untruthfully, that in his films he always got the girl even if, sometimes, it was not until after the cameras had stopped rolling.

Among the targets of his attentions was actress Shelley Winters, herself no stranger to off-screen love affairs, who recalled their romance in vivid detail in her autobiography. She also reflected on the end of the affair which came when she read in the newspapers that Norma was expecting their fifth child. She told Marlon Brando, with whom she was about to start a relationship, 'I know in my heart it's true; that bastard's fucking his wife.'

When Shelley was briefly hospitalized as a result of the emotional stress she suffered, Lancaster sent her roses and a cheque for $3,000. 'I told him to keep the roses but I kept the $3,000 – my severance pay, I guess.'

Lancaster's collaboration with Harold Hecht was also enjoying an exciting time with another off-beat production, *The Bachelor Party* (1957), which was written by Paddy Chayefsky (who had written *Marty*). However, despite its quality, the film did rather badly. Stories about ordinary people doing ordinary things often miss the target – the attention of ordinary men and women – and this one was not the exception the producers had hoped it would be.

In contrast to his off-screen life, Lancaster must have found the setting of his next two films – the west – rather tame. Settings apart, these films were very different in all other respects.

The Rainmaker (1956) does not hide its origins as a tightly constrained television drama (which had also been presented on the stage before it reached the big screen). Using a compact set and restricted movement, the potential dangers of 'staginess' are largely overcome by the lyrical flow of the dialogue. Written (in all three conceptions) by N. Richard Nash, the story centres upon Starbuck (Lancaster) an itinerant con man who drifts into a small Kansas community in 1913 where he proceeds to charm into a swan the ugly duckling daughter of a poor farmer.

The young woman is Lizzie Curry (Katharine Hepburn) who believes only in harsh reality, epitomized by the drought-afflicted land upon which her family scratches an arid living and her own appearance which she believes to be dull and dowdy.

The garrulous Starbuck convinces her of the value of dreams while simultaneously trying to con the family out of a hundred dollars, in return for which he claims that he will bring rain to end the drought that threatens ruin.

Gradually, the torrent of words melts Lizzie's resistance to dreams and she is persuaded that she possesses inner beauty. She effects a compromise, accepting that there is room in her life for Starbuck's dreams, but she stops short of agreeing to join him on his wanderings. Instead, she elects to stay behind, now aglow with her new-found appreciation of her once-hidden beauty and plans to marry her patient suitor, Deputy Sheriff File (Wendell Corey).

As Starbuck drives his horse and wagon out of the farmyard the rains come, proving to Lizzie that sometimes even dreams can come true.

All principal roles in *The Rainmaker* are well executed, with Hepburn achieving that most difficult of feats as she evolves from plainness to beauty by little more than the expression in her eyes. For his part, Lancaster brings to the con man a believable gift for spinning webs of relatively harmless deceit with an endless and delightful stream of words.

The two stars got on well with one another, after a frosty start brought about by a rare instance of unprofessionalism by Lancaster. Late on the set on the first day of shooting, he was roundly castigated by Hepburn and was his usual punctual self thereafter.

Although set in the west, *The Rainmaker* was not a western, but Lancaster's next film was very much the real thing belonging as it did to the breed of big-budget horse operas that proliferated through the late 1950s and early sixties. In fact, he later asserted that he hadn't wanted to make *Gunfight at the OK Corral* (1957) because he thought the script too talky, but agreed to it when, in return, Hal Wallis allowed him to do *The Rainmaker*.

Gunfight at the OK Corral was one of several Hollywood versions of the exploits of real-life lawman Wyatt Earp. Like all the others, this one limited itself to a small but colourfully violent page in Earp's somewhat dubious history. As usual where bio-pics are concerned, Hollywood showed little interest in the truth. Since any reading of Earp's story (which the man himself actively promoted with scant regard for the truth) provides enough material for a dozen films, his mistreatment by film-makers is inexplicable.

Here, the screenplay concentrates upon events leading up to the most famous gunfight in the West's bloody history and upon the strange friendship between Wyatt Earp (Lancaster) and Doc Holliday (Kirk Douglas). In real life this friendship was not as steadfast as is shown on the screen. The homicidal and consumptive dentist's insistence on following Earp around the country was due more to an acute sense of self-preservation than because he liked the lawman. Doc had once helped Earp out of a tight spot and hence hoped that he was less likely to lock him up for his frequent indiscretions than were most other law-officers along the frontier.

Lancaster's Earp is characterized as a strong but good-natured individual who prefers the quiet life, unless provoked into action by determined efforts on the part of the ungodly.

In many such confrontations, Earp is supported by one or more of his gun-toting, badge-wearing brothers including Morgan (DeForrest Kelley) and Virgil (John Hudson).

Doc Holliday, who has developed addictions to drink and cards, is also called into service when Earp goes up against the Clanton gang, a mixed bag of villains and unwashed layabouts including brothers Ike and Billy Clanton (Lyle Bettger and Dennis Hopper).

The West of motion pictures was always very much a man's world and this film is no exception. The women involved are all minor characters. Ma Clanton, matriarch of the evil gang, is played by Olive Carey, widow of Harry Carey, the great star of bygone Hollywood westerns. The glamour comes in the shape of a somewhat reserved and stately lady named Laura Denbow (Rhonda Fleming), who neither looks nor sounds like the gambler she's supposed to be, and Kate Fisher (Jo Van Fleet), Doc Holliday's lady-love.

From the names given to these fictional ladies it might be inferred that they owe their origins to the two long-standing lady-friends Doc Holliday had in real life, a pretty gambler named Lottie Deno and a whore with the unprepossessing name of Big Nose Kate Elder.

The gunfight at the end of the film is well staged, and if it bears no resemblance to reality this divergence from the truth can be justified on the grounds that real gunfights in the Old West were short and curiously static affairs. Apart from which, nineteenth-century hand-guns were notoriously inaccurate and most gunfighters would have had difficulty hitting a barn even if they were inside it.

A later film, *Doc* (1971), had the combatants stand almost nose-to-nose and compacted the OK shoot-out into seven seconds of screentime, probably about the duration of the real thing. Reality, however, doesn't always pay off.

Having given the film its title, the makers wouldn't have dared wind up the fireworks in just seven seconds. They would've been lynched. For once, maybe, tinkering with history was justified – if only on the grounds of self-preservation.

In the event, the athletic, smoke-filled, bullet-ridden extravaganza choreographed by director John Sturges in *Gunfight at the OK Corral* gave the fans their money's worth, and then some.

The film is full of strong supporting players including Frank Faylen as turncoat Sheriff Cotton Wilson, Lee Van Cleef as Ed

Bailey, Earl Holliman as Charles Bassett, and the always excellent and usually underrated John Ireland as Ringo.

For all the strength of the supporting players, the nature of the script allows the two leads to run away with the acting honours. Kirk Douglas turns in a suitably bravura performance as the malevolent dentist, even though he looks much too healthy for an alcoholic consumptive (but not as healthy as Victor Mature who played the role in an earlier version of the tale).

Lancaster gives Earp a depth of character that admirably fits this version of the lawman's life, even if, in reality, he was an unsavoury liar who acted almost as much on the wrong side of the law as he did in its name.

In the *New York Times*, Bosley Crowther had mellowed enough to be moderately complimentary about the film without singling out too many people for individual praise. 'It is all very obvious, but it is very active. Things happen all through the film (except at those odd, embarrassing moments when Cupid lets fly with his arrows). It is firmly directed by John Sturges, and it is ruggedly acted by all and sundry – of which there is quite a heap.'

Lancaster's self-esteem surfaced during the filming of *Gunfight at the OK Corral* when he persistently argued with director Sturges until eventually he was allowed to perform a scene he had rewritten to his own liking. That done, he got on with the job, and apparently never noticed that 'his' scene failed to appear in the finished film.

Interviewed by Gordon Gow, Lancaster later observed, 'I was constantly worrying about the writing of the scripts I acted in. I was always wanting to change the staging of scenes, always feeling it could be done in a different way. I never lost that tendency. For some reason many directors find it difficult to work with me.' Maybe they hadn't been smart enough to do as Sturges had done and take steps which appeared to let the star have his head while actually retaining complete control of the film.

The location filming of *Gunfight at the OK Corral* in Arizona gave Lancaster and Douglas the opportunity to develop their friendship, although it can't have been an easy ride. On one occasion, onlookers observed Douglas was reduced to tears

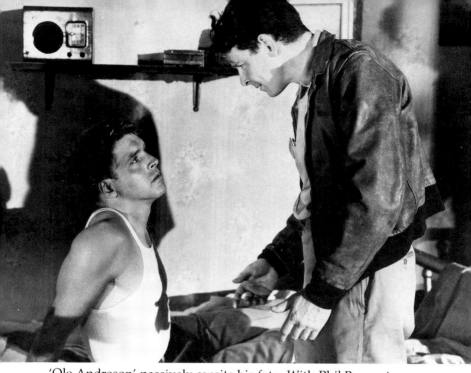

'Ole Andreson' passively awaits his fate. With Phil Brown in
The Killers (1946)

Counting off the days. 'Joe Collins' with Howard Duff in
Brute Force (1947)

'Steve Thompson'
defending Yvonne De
Carlo, who will lead him
to death in *Criss Cross*
(1949)

'Dardo the Arrow'
prepares to right wrongs
in *The Flame and The Arrow*
(1950)

Publicity play with an unnamed dog

(*Below*) 'Sergeant Milt Warden' with Deborah Kerr as anger replaces passion after their steamy beach scene in *From Here to Eternity* (1953)

Relaxing with Kirk
Douglas on the set of
Gunfight at the OK Corral
(1957)

10209-2/60

Once an acrobat . . . with Nick Cravat

'Elmer Gantry' preaching fire and brimstone from the pulpit in
Elmer Gantry (1960)

'J. J. Hunsecker' at the centre of his evil web. With Tony Curtis
in *Sweet Smell of Success* (1957)

On-screen disharmony between 'Hank Bell' and Shelley
Winters in *The Young Savages* (1961)

(Left) 'Robert Stroud' captive with his caged birds in *Birdman of Alcatraz* (1962)

(Centre) Relaxing in opulent splendour as, outside, the world changes, 'Don Fabrizio, Prince of Salina' contemplates the future with Claudia Cardinale and Alain Delon in *The Leopard* (1963)

(Foot of page) 'General James M. Scott' turns his back on the man he seeks to overthrow in *Seven Days in May* (1964)

'Bill Dolworth' in fighting mood in *The Professionals* (1966)
(*Below*) 'Ned Merrill' prepares to set out on a personal odyssey
that will lead to tragic disappointment in *The Swimmer* (1968)

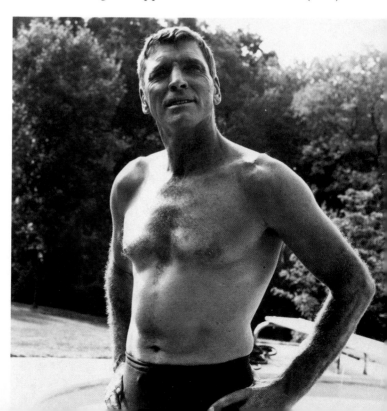

when Lancaster urged autograph-seeking fans who were surrounding him to ask Douglas for his, telling them that he was a great performer before adding, 'Of course, you don't recognize him without his built-up shoes.'

From underplaying the larger-than-life, wide open spaces character of Wyatt Earp, Lancaster, having fulfilled the expectations of his fans by strapping on a six-shooter, appeared in a challenging film. In this he tackled a difficult role as a powerful and menacing individual whose habitat was beneath any available and preferably slimy urban stone.

In *Sweet Smell of Success* (1957), J.J. Hunsecker (Lancaster) is a monomaniacal newspaper columnist who lurks menacingly at the centre of a web of deceit and corruption. His gossip column can make or break, and it is the breaking that Hunsecker sees as his mission in life, mercilessly hounding in print men and women whose only sins are to have offended his confused morality.

The one redeeming feature in Hunsecker's life is his sister Susan (Susan Harrison), but even her image is soiled by the incestuous attachment he feels for her.

Susan is seeing a young guitarist, Steve Dallas (Martin Milner), and in an attempt to break up the romance (for no other reason than to remove another man from his sister's life) Hunsecker seeks to destroy Steve. His tool in this enterprise is Sidney Falco (Tony Curtis), a publicity agent who desperately wants to see his clients' names in Hunsecker's influential column.

Falco is obliged to plant items that imply Steve is both a drug addict and a communist (at the time of the film either fact would have severely damaged any artist's career, both would have wiped him out of existence). The ploy fails and Hunsecker discovers that his sister is unrepentantly prepared to continue seeing Steve. Hunsecker decides that Steve must go to prison, and to achieve this he asks Falco to plant marijuana on the guitarist before notifying the police, and as an encouragement to the publicity agent promises that he can take over the column as guest editor while Hunsecker takes a three-month vacation with Susan.

This time the plan works but Falco's joy is short-lived. Called to Hunsecker's apartment he finds Susan, half-naked and suicidal. When Hunsecker arrives, he believes that Falco has tried to rape the girl. Hunsecker throws him out and calls the police, telling them not only that Falco has planted false evidence on Steve, but that he no longer enjoys his protection.

The police, who tread softly around the columnist and his sycophantic entourage, need no diagrams; it is open season on the egregious Falco.

But Hunsecker has gone too far in his attempt to hold on to his sister. She has seen his true, evil nature, and she packs her bags and leaves. Ironically enough, Hunsecker achieves his objective because Susan goes not to join Steve but alone. These events have given her the strength and determination to live her own life now.

Sweet Smell of Success marked a visual and schematic return to *film noir*, but with differences wrought by the passage of time. The film is a compelling study of deception, corruption and emotional dishonesty. Susan and Steve apart, the characters on view display few moral scruples and everyone, Susan and Steve included, loses. Despite the film's title, success is unattainable for these sink-dwellers. Indeed, this marks one major difference from earlier *films noirs* in that there is no one here with whom the audience can identify.

For the amoral Hunsecker, people are pawns to be manipulated for his own sadistic amusement; even his sister, for whom he professes love, is used to serve his ends. Falco is cold-blooded towards everyone and is too far gone in his depravity to realize that through his behaviour to others he is digging his own grave. Even the amiable Steve loses out, although innocent of everything of which he has been accused and guilty only of being too soft and easily manipulated.

Stylistically and in its direction, acting and photography, *Sweet Smell of Success* can scarcely be faulted, yet it drew much less acclaim than latter-day screenings suggest it warrants. Perhaps it showed a side of show business which audiences and critics (some of whom could doubtless discern glimmers of themselves in J.J. Hunsecker) were not yet ready to accept.

Some of the film's acidity undoubtedly springs from the original screenplay, written by Ernest Lehman from his own novella. His script was given a little dialogue-polishing by Clifford Odets and the collaboration generated some marvellous touches. It is hard to think of many other Hollywood writers who would have given Hunsecker a line like: 'Sidney lives ... in marled twilight.' Then there is the masterly line near the film's end when the corrupt cop, Harry Kello (Emile Meyer), calls to the suddenly unprotected Falco, 'Come back, Sidney. I want to chastise you.' The line, as written and to a great extent as delivered, is filled with menacing sado-homosexual undertones which admirably suit the relationship between the two men.

The director of *Sweet Smell of Success*, Scottish film-maker Alexander MacKendrick, seems at first glance an improbable choice for this kind of film. His credits in Britain included such calculated and very British whimsy as *Whisky Galore* (1949), *The Man in the White Suit* (1951) and *The Ladykillers* (1955).

Talking to Derek Malcolm of the *Guardian* in 1972, Lancaster recalled the making of *Sweet Smell of Success* and particularly MacKendrick's measured approach to his job.

> Sandy was a very clever director, and a very nice guy. But he took one helluva lot of time. He would get hold a scene that was five-and-a-half pages long and attempt to do it in one take by moving the dolley around and through the characters – an incredibly difficult task. We would arrive on the set ready to go at nine in the morning and we'd be hanging around till three in the afternoon rehearsing the moves we had to make. Then we'd shoot, and sometimes he'd say: 'No, I don't like that much. Let's do it a different way'.

However disconcerting the director's technique might have been, the cast appears not to have been thrown. Without exception, the acting throughout is never less than good and is often quite remarkable.

Among the minor roles brought to vivid if unpleasant life are those played by Sam Levene, Barbara Nichols (very touching as the hooker Falco will not allow to break free of her grim lifestyle) and Emile Meyer.

Tony Curtis seized eagerly upon his first opportunity to escape the stereotyping to which his dark good looks had doomed him early in his career and in many respects it is his film. The greasy charm he gives to Falco is exactly right.

As the bespectacled, spiderlike J.J. Hunsecker, Lancaster once again underplays, rightly giving the character disturbing undercurrents of evil. Handled badly the role could have been unbalanced either way: to overheated melodrama, or to develop an edge of sympathy for Hunsecker when he loses the one thing he holds dear.

At the end, as Susan is about to walk out on her brother, she tells him, 'I'd rather be dead than living with you. For all the things you've done, J.J., I should hate you but I don't. I pity you.'

It is a measure of the manner in which Lancaster plays the role that the audience doesn't pity Hunsecker one little bit.

Off screen in 1957, Lancaster was deeply involved in the complexities of the motion-picture business. Once again, his production company had changed its name. This time, to accommodate the fact that James Hill had become a full partner, the company was known as Hecht–Hill–Lancaster. In January 1957, the Screenwriters branch of the Writers Guild of America (West) considered strike action against the company because of its alleged refusal to negotiate in collective bargaining agreements.

In the same month, writer John van Druten sued for $90,000, allegedly the unpaid portion of a contract for a rejected screenplay, later settling out of court for $70,000.

More legal actions followed in July, this time when the tussles over the origins of *Trapeze* were complicated by Hecht–Lancaster's suing Sophia Loren for $350,000, claiming they had retained her services for two films, a claim which she denied.

It was doubtless with some relief that Lancaster was able to submerge himself in another film, this time a straightforward underwater war story.

Run Silent, Run Deep (1958) concentrates on the conflict generated in a US Navy submarine during World War II when a new man, Commander Richardson (Clark Gable) is given command of USS *Nerka* over the head of the executive officer, Lieutenant Bledsoe (Lancaster), who thinks that he should have had the job.

Matters on board are aggravated by Richardson's disciplinarian attitude which leads to the sinking of a Japanese destroyer. The men are unsettled when they realize that Richardson is fighting his own war, intent on avenging the loss of his last command.

When Richardson is injured, Bledsoe takes charge and in the ensuing action the commander is killed.

Fairly routine war fare though it is, the film has its moments thanks largely to strong playing from the two main actors both of whom not only act the part but look as if they could well be tough submariners.

In an article in *Focus on Film* in 1973, director Robert Wise recalled the production as being one beset by troubles. 'We had a lot of problems with the script before we started – getting something we could all agree on. Then as we were shooting, there was a lot of behind-the-scenes fighting and pulling going on between the three partners in the company (Hecht, Hill and Lancaster), and the writer, John Gay, was right in the middle ... '

Although both of Lancaster's remaining two films of the 1950s originated in transatlantic stage plays, they were very different affairs, even if both achieved a similar lack of distinction when brought to the screen.

Separate Tables (1958) was adapted by Terence Rattigan and John Gay from Rattigan's stage success and was strongly cast with Deborah Kerr, Gladys Cooper, Wendy Hiller and David Niven (who won an Oscar as Best Supporting Actor for his role as Major Pollock, the self-proclaimed war hero who is in fact a phoney and a molester of women to boot).

Originally, Laurence Olivier had been cast in the role taken by Niven, but he and Lancaster clashed; quite clearly, the film wasn't big enough for both of them, and as Lancaster was co-producer it was Olivier who quit.

The closely observed private lives of the residents at a Bournemouth boarding-house was strange territory for both Lancaster and his co-star, Rita Hayworth (who married James Hill during the making of the film), but they emerged without too much dishonour, even if the style of Rattigan's writing and the setting gave the British supporting players a substantial edge over the Americans.

The differences between Lancaster and Olivier were smoothed over for *The Devil's Disciple* (1959), written for the screen by John Dighton and Roland Kibbee from the stage play by George Bernard Shaw.

Set in New England during the American War of Independence, the film cast Kirk Douglas as the rebellious Dick Dudgeon, Laurence Olivier as General Burgoyne, and Burt

Lancaster as Anthony Anderson, a stuffed-shirt pastor.

Uneven and with a mixed bag of acting techniques, the film, which is set in a period which always seems to trouble film-makers, ended the decade on a low note.

Nevertheless, the 1950s had seen Lancaster constantly searching for demanding roles that ran the entire gamut of Hollywood's need for genre identification. Only rarely were his characters two-dimensional sketches. He always sought, and usually found, depths that were sometimes not put there by screenwriters.

He had also enjoyed close brushes with the Academy Awards, especially with *From Here to Eternity*, and he had helped co-stars Shirley Booth and Anna Magnani to win Best Actress Oscars. In these and other films he saw work in which he appeared bring flurries of the statuettes to others. He was also co-producer of *Marty*, the surprise 1955 winner as Best Film, but his own personal Oscar still eluded him.

It was something that would not elude him much longer.

5   An Oscar for Elmer

At the start of the 1960s, more than ever before in his career, Burt Lancaster was reluctant to take on roles in which he had no belief or for which he had no feeling. True, he would continue to make movies from time to time just for the money, but, as he observed to journalists, he had a large and happy family and was rich enough to indulge his passion for the arts. (Fortunately, his valuable collection of paintings was on loan to a gallery when his rambling California home was destroyed in the disastrous Bel-Air fire of 1961.)

At the close of the 1950s, Lancaster's independence had led him to turn down the title role in *Ben Hur* for reasons stemming from his disapproval of the screenplay's insistence that Christianity was the one and only true religion. His childhood background had shown him that the beliefs of many of his fellow countrymen ran counter to the Christian faith. Even if he had no compelling religious belief of his own, he felt that to portray the character as written was inherently false.

In the event, the role went to the actor who was to have played the supporting role of Messala, Charlton Heston (who had once been touted as 'a new Burt Lancaster', only to draw the sour response from Hal B. Wallis, 'Yes, but do we *need* a new Burt Lancaster?').

Just as Lancaster's conscience was troubled at this time, so too was the American nation's although for a very different reason. The national conscience had been belatedly stricken by recognition of the appalling treatment in the nineteenth century of Native Americans, the 'Red Indians'. The actions of the white man of those times had bordered upon genocide and now some way of demonstrating an acceptance of guilt was being sought.

The American film industry, which had spent almost half a

71

century compounding earlier errors by portraying the Native American as a painted savage, had begun to make amends with such mid-1950s films as *Broken Arrow* and Lancaster's own *Apache*.

Almost overnight, filmgoers found themselves subjected to muddled philosophizing from film-makers whose products often cast serious doubt on their motives; unless they hoped that making a movie with a message was a way of ensuring a place in heaven while simultaneously generating enough money to allow them to enjoy the good life here on earth.

The Native American as an object of racism became almost as much a stock figure as his earlier 'painted savage' counterpart. The possibly well-intentioned aims of films like *Apache* were assiduously pursued by film-makers, good, bad and ugly.

Lancaster ventured into one such tale directed by John Huston, whose personal attitude on racial and religious matters was frequently questionable.

Based upon a novel by Alan le May, *The Unforgiven* (1960) relates the problems besetting a group of white settlers in the Texas Panhandle at odds with a band of Kiowas.

Ben Zachary (Lancaster) runs a ranch which also supports his mother Mattilda (Lillian Gish), his brothers Cash and Andy (Audie Murphy and Doug McClure), his partner Zeb Rawlins (Charles Bickford), and a young woman named Rachel (Audrey Hepburn).

It is Rachel's origins which form the hub of the film's dark tale of racial bigotry and bitterness. Rachel is a Native American who was adopted by Ben's father when her family was massacred by members of a hostile tribe – the Kiowas.

When the other whites learn the truth about Rachel, they isolate the Zacharys and the girl becomes a helpless pawn for whom everyone devises a fate to suit his own ends. Only Ben stands by her; and is justified when Rachel proves her worthiness to remain a member of white society through the dubious expedient of sending her real brother to the happy hunting-ground.

Lancaster is sound in his central role, but his character's grimly obsessive determination to defend Rachel against Kiowas, settlers, his brother, her brother, and just about everyone within a day's ride of the old homestead, suggests that an interesting plot element lay unmined just beneath the surface of the script.

Well-photographed by Franz Planer, the film did little for the reputation of John Huston who collected some of the worst press notices of his long, usually distinguished but occasionally deeply flawed, career.

Bigotry was a central factor in Lancaster's next film, but it was about a different sort of bigot and the result was vastly superior being clear-headed, skilful and distinguished in its aims, methods and results.

Elmer Gantry (1960) takes a hard swipe at religious bigotry, revivalism, hypocrisy and the gullibility of the populace. In particular, it exposes the tendency of many Americans to allow themselves to be caught up and whirled along in pursuit of salvation by silver-tongued demagogues.

Gantry (Lancaster) is a travelling salesman, down on his luck, who is attracted to Sister Sharon Falconer (Jean Simmons) when he wanders into one of her revivalist meetings. A former divinity student, expelled for seducing a church elder's daughter, Gantry persuades Sister Sharon to let him join her organization. Displaying a pyrotechnical style of oratory, Gantry builds up a sizeable following in the Bible Belt states and wins Sister Sharon's unqualified support and fatally uncritical love.

The caution of Sister Sharon's colleague William L. Morgan (Dean Jagger) and the hostile scepticism of journalist Jim Lefferts (Arthur Kennedy) create tensions, which are forced to the surface when the evangelists are invited to move their crusade out of the sticks and into the city.

In the city, where Sharon hopes to build a tabernacle, Gantry meets up with the girl he seduced long ago. Lulu Bains (Shirley Jones) is now a prostitute and it is through her that Gantry is exposed for the mountebank he really is.

The unfinished tabernacle is destroyed by a fire in which Sister Sharon dies. Gantry's claims as a leader of men's souls have been displayed as a sham; but he ends with a measure of self-discovery. What matters, he now believes, is for a man to determine what is right for *him*, rather than to take as the gospel-truth what others decree to be right.

Based upon Sinclair Lewis's novel, Richard Brooks's screenplay is finely crafted. Much of the indigestibility of

Lewis's work disappears (he usually took massive, complex subjects for his themes and wrote massive chunks of complex prose about them) and the satirical content is more surely aimed. Brooks also directed and he maintained a powerful combination of imaginative visual imagery and swirling clouds of words from beginning to end.

Every role, from lead to the smallest of bit-part players, is convincingly cast and superbly acted. As Sister Sharon, Jean Simmons is vulnerable and sincere. Dean Jagger, as Sharon's older and supposedly wiser mentor, skilfully displays genuine religious conviction undercut by his mercenary approval of the financial benefits Gantry brings to their movement.

Arthur Kennedy's cynical newshound is yet another in a long string of fine supporting roles played by this unacclaimed actor. Shirley Jones was cast against type as the prostitute and as a result her role of good-girl-turned-bad is given strength.

Academy Awards went to Jones, as Best Supporting Actress, and to Brooks for Best Screenplay. The film's third Oscar went to Burt Lancaster.

On screen almost throughout, from the saloon where he exhorts his fellow salesmen to adopt the wild life, to walking barefoot along the railroad track from where he enters a church to join the hymn-singing of a black congregation, and on through the free-wheeling, acrobatic razzmatazz of his fire-and-brimstone preaching, Lancaster's performance is a joy.

The pathetic hopelessness with which the poor and the afflicted flock to Gantry's ever more outrageous sermons is made believable because the actor makes his character entirely convincing. Anyone, the sick, the ill-educated, and especially those like Sharon who *want* to believe, cannot help but be taken in by his magnetic personality, overwhelming self-confidence and brash charm. (Lancaster cheerfully acknowledges that the role was one of the easiest he has played: 'I was, in essence, playing myself'.)

What makes this performance a great one is the manner in which Gantry's eventual reversal – his moment of self-discovery – is made to seem completely natural and within character. Gantry is supposed to end as a different man, but his change is dictated by external developments and his new self-awareness. The basic character of the man, his powerful, cocksure, extrovert charm, remains unaltered and is thus made stronger. As indicated by John Cutts, writing in *Films and Filming* in January 1961, Lancaster 'manages to convey this character change splendidly. His performance is a glorious mixture of natural personality and applied characterization, and the result makes for a telling and notable piece of screen acting.'

After Gantry, any role Lancaster tackled was faced with an inevitable sense of anti-climax and there is certainly a subdued air about *The Young Savages* (1961).

This film brought Lancaster into contact with John Frankenheimer, a young television director with whom he was to make four films in as many years.

A tough, grittily realistic story, based upon an Evan Hunter novel, *The Young Savages* has Lancaster as an assistant district attorney struggling to combat juvenile crime in the slums of New York City. As much a statement of social conscience as a crime drama, the film did Lancaster no harm and ensured that Frankenheimer would stay in films.

Next, Lancaster made *Judgement at Nuremberg* (1961). Based upon the television play by Abby Mann, who also scripted the film version, this is an overlong, fictionalized account of the war crimes trials which followed World War II.

It is an undoubtedly well-intentioned attempt to explore the problem of individual responsibility for the actions of the state, but it is frequently ponderous.

An all-star cast, many of whom worked for next to nothing in order to make a public statement of personal belief through their roles, included Montgomery Clift, Marlene Dietrich, Judy Garland, Spencer Tracy, Maximilian Schell and Richard Widmark.

As one of the accused, initially grimly unrepentant of his wartime activities, Lancaster gives an assured if somewhat mannered portrayal of chilling idealism turned rancid by nationalistic and racist fervour.

Judgement at Nuremberg's chief flaw lies in the occasionally sledge-hammer touch of both writing and direction. The cold monochrome of the picture is matched by the simplistic right or wrong of many of the characterizations.

Nothing done by the Nazis can be justified but, as later film-makers proved, it can be revealing for an audience to learn *why* men and nations behaved as did Hitler and his rabid gang. Piling one appalling fact upon another does not necessarily lead to understanding; yet it is understanding which is most important for this may lead towards an ability to recognize danger signals long before it is too late to act.

Initially, the National Socialist movement in Germany gained support among intellectuals and idealists as well as vicious racists and mindless bigots. To combat future attempts to revive the spirit of extreme nationalism something more is needed than the occasionally stereotyped sketching supplied in *Judgement at Nuremberg*.

Fine performances abounded in the film resulting in four Academy Award nominations and a further six nominations among non-acting categories. Only Maximilian Schell, as Best Actor, and Abby Mann, for his screenplay, were successful.

Burt Lancaster's withdrawn, considered performance as Ernst Janning was to result in a positive benefit for him. Italian film producer Goffredo Lombardo saw *Judgement at Nuremberg* while on a visit to New York and was sufficiently impressed to argue with Luchino Visconti that Lancaster was much more than a player of gangsters and cowboys. His argument was so convincing that it led to Lancaster's working in Italy on a Visconti masterpiece. Before that association, however, there was time for two more film roles (plus a cameo appearance) of which the first was anything but makeweight.

For *Birdman of Alcatraz* (1962) Lancaster was reunited with director John Frankenheimer in the extraordinary but true story of Robert Stroud.

Sentenced in 1909 to twelve years in prison for killing a man, any chances Stroud (Lancaster) might have had for parole vanished when his violent temper led him to attack a fellow inmate. Classified as unregenerate, Stroud suffers severe restrictions, among which is the authorities' refusal to allow his mother to see him when she travels hundreds of miles only to arrive on a non-visiting day. Stroud, his temper once more out of control, fights with a prison guard who dies in the struggle.

Sentenced to death for this crime, Stroud is saved when his mother Elizabeth (Thelma Ritter) successfully petitions President Woodrow Wilson.

His sentence commuted to imprisonment for life in solitary,

Stroud becomes even more alienated, but the chance discovery in the prison yard of a fledgling fallen from its nest changes his life.

He cares for the baby bird, sees it recover, and gradually acquires more birds. His interest in his tiny charges leads him to become an expert on avian diseases, eventually writing a book which becomes the classic textbook on the subject.

A prize-winning article he writes for a magazine leads him into friendship and a business relationship with Stella Johnson (Betty Field) whom he marries thanks to a technical loophole in the law. These actions irritate the authorities and, after a brief flurry of public interest in his case has died down, Stroud is abruptly transferred to Alcatraz.

No longer able to keep birds (the title should really have been *Birdman of Leavenworth*), Stroud writes another book – this time about caged men – but is refused permission to have it published. During the 1946 riot on Alcatraz his actions help save lives but still he receives no parole.

In 1959, half a century after he entered prison, Stroud is transferred to a prison hospital. Alhough still not free, he is at last out of solitary confinement.

Necessarily, much of the film is static and claustrophobically enclosed yet despite this and its length there is little feeling of inaction. Much of the credit for this lies in Frankenheimer's taut direction and a controlled, introspective performance from Lancaster which proved to be yet another of his infinitely varied depictions of men of inner strength barely shrouded in gentleness.

After the early stages of the film, during which the character displays an almost psychopathic propensity for violence, Lancaster brought to Robert Stroud a measure of dignity and humanity that may well have been absent in the real person.

During the filming of *Birdman of Alcatraz*, Lancaster's ability to compartmentalize his private and professional life was demonstrated when his brother Jim, who was working on the set as an assistant to the director, suffered a fatal heart attack. Whatever grief he might have felt for the brother who had helped support the family during their early days in New York, Lancaster insisted that they should work on.

Other main roles in *Birdman of Alcatraz* received varied

treatment. Throughout her career, Thelma Ritter frequently slid over into exaggerated sentimentality with her stock-in-trade of golden-hearted ladies with tongues like buzz-saws. This was no place for a wisecracking caricature and, while she was able to restrain herself from the habit, the strain shows, and she is often uneasy. Neville Brand and Karl Malden both turn in sound performances as representatives of law and order, but most credit among the supporting players went deservedly to Telly Savalas in the role of fellow prisoner Feto Gomez who, for a while, shared Stroud's passion for birds. Savalas, still many years away from the self-congratulatory stereotyping he employed in his tele- vision series *Kojak*, was nominated for and won the Academy Award as Best Supporting Actor. (Lancaster was also an Oscar nominee, as Best Actor, but lost to Gregory Peck who won for his role in *To Kill a Mocking-bird*.)

From concern for men incarcerated for criminal acts, Lancas- ter's next role saw him involved with others shut away from the sight of a seemingly uncaring society.

Based by Abby Mann upon his own television play, *A Child is Waiting* (1963) is a story of the problems facing staff and patients at a hospital for mentally disturbed children.

The superintendant of the hospital is Dr Matthew Clark (Lancaster), a stern and sometimes apparently unsympathetic individual. He gains a new member of staff in the shape of Jean Hansen (Judy Garland), who appears almost as unstable as the patients. Miss Hansen is an emotional and over-sensitive young woman, employed to teach music, who lets her own hang-ups interfere with her work and unwisely focuses much of her time and attention upon one particular child. He is Reuben Widdi- combe (Bruce Ritchey) who, although outwardly normal, has deep-seated psychiatric problems generated by his parents (Steve Hill and Gena Rowlands).

Eventually, Miss Hansen is persuaded to see that her duty lies not in imposing her own solutions or shielding the children with love but in helping them find within themselves the limited, often negligible, capacity to cope with their situation. She also learns that Matthew Clark's stern exterior conceals a kind and caring heart.

The film walks an uneasy tightrope between documentary directness and soft sentimentality, often with soggily predictable results. The fact that director John Cassavetes was rarely guilty of sentimentality suggests that he was hampered by the producers who had their eyes on the film's commercial possibilities.

Such considerations are evidenced by the decision to cast Bruce Ritchey in the film's key role. His performance is solid, but he is a normal boy, an actor playing a role, while all around him the other patients are youngsters with real mental ailments recruited from Pacific State Hospital in Pomona, California. The documentary impression created by the presence of these patients is undercut by the use in their midst of someone who can, at the end of the day's shooting, wipe away his problems along with his make-up and go on home.

The adult cast all perform creditably and with credibility. However, there is a lingering impression that here was a motion-picture which could have advanced concern for the treatment of people with mental disorders, but which was sabotaged by the very individuals who had the courage to decide to make it in the first place.

Saturday Review commented that it was wonderful how the stars had worked alongside the children. 'Miss Garland and Lancaster radiate a warmth so genuine that one is certain that the children are responding directly to them, not merely following some vaguely comprehended script.' Certainly, Lancaster's later insistence that he was not generally at ease when working with children is not apparent here.

Lancaster's personal commitment to causes not necessarily in line with those popular with the general public extended to more than merely the making of films such as *A Child is Waiting*. During 1963, while filming in Paris, he flew back to America for one day so that he could join in Martin Luther King's march on Washington.

Set against such acts, the cameo role Lancaster played in John Huston's undistinguished suspense thriller, *The List of Adrian Messenger* (1963) seems an even greater mistake than it appeared on the screen. Along with Tony Curtis, Frank Sinatra and Robert Mitchum, he appeared heavily made up as part of a running gag intended to keep audiences in their seats. A kitful of red herrings tries the same things as Kirk Douglas, wearing a succession of latex face masks, kills off anyone in his way to inheriting a fortune.

Lancaster was in drag as a female anti-blood sports campaigner in tweed suit, sensible brogues and headscarf and would have certainly frightened the jodhpurs off even the hardiest master of fox hounds but the joke – if that is what it was – was thin and didn't help overcome the film's built-in weariness.

The contrast between this exercise in trivia and Lancaster's next film role was wider than the gulf of centuries. From being disguised by the make-up man's artifice, he used his own art to thoroughly immerse himself in a part which was the greatest test and ultimately the greatest triumph of his career up to this date – even if, when first screened in an ineptly-edited version, this was not readily apparent to audiences.

The Leopard (1963) was based upon the novel by a genuine nobleman albeit an amateur writer. It was brought to the screen by Luchino Visconti, an artist of film-making but a man for whom commercial success outside Italy never seemed to be particularly important.

The disintegration of powerful families as a result of changing times, shifts in political alliances and the inherent degeneration caused by a reluctance to admit new and possibly less noble blood, is a theme to which Visconti returned on a number of occasions, beginning in 1960 with *Rocco and his Brothers*.

In *The Leopard*, he traces the attempts of an ageing aristocrat to restore his family's ebbing fortunes by encouraging his nephew to marry the daughter of the newly-rich but lower-class mayor of a Sicilian village.

Set against the political background of Italy in ferment as the old order (the Bourbon state) gives way under violent revolution to the new (Garibaldi and his followers), the nobleman's marriage-broking activities might appear wayward, but he knows what he's doing. He knows that all political change is superficial and that underneath everything will remain the way it is. Garibaldi is a passing phase and what the aristocrat and his family must do (together with ruling classes everywhere) is gracefully concede the minimum amount of change necessary to convince revolutionaries that they have won their hard-sought victories. In reality, the nobleman knows, such victories are illusory; revolutions come and go but the old order remains forever. The Risorgimento is only the latest, and will be by no means the last, of Italy's attempts to revive its former glories.

The story of an aristocrat's gentle bowing before the wind of change may seem a thin thread on which to hang a very long film (over three hours), but this is concerned with more than individual human endeavours. What mattered to Visconti (and the original novelist) was that a portrait should emerge of a nation under change at a critical moment in its history. Both Visconti and the novelist, Giuseppe Tomasi di Lampedusa, succeed in painting such a portrait, but the end result is not one but two portraits.

Visconti's vision is elegaic, a thing of romantic beauty superbly executed; Lampedusa's was wart-ridden.

In the film's original form, which hardly anyone was allowed to see at the time of its first release, Visconti's view was the better for eschewing reality in favour of sumptuous elegance. As it appeared in 1963, roughly cut and cut again, poorly dubbed, and with even its colour process changed, Visconti's vision was destroyed.

In an article in the *Sunday Times* on 27 Ocober 1963, Visconti wrote that in his opinion the version prepared for the American market was 'badly cut and dubbed with ill-chosen, unsuitable voices.' He also asserted that the result was 'processed as if it were a bright piece of Hollywoodiana' and he even 'had difficulty in following the plot'. Not surprisingly he claimed it to be a 'work for which I acknowledge no paternity at all'.

It is tempting to speculate that Visconti might have been better advised to have gone for reality, thus giving the distributors less to damage but, fortunately, listening to advice was not one of his characteristics and the film world is the better for it.

A few perceptive commentators saw through the film's mistreatment, some thanks to having seen it at Cannes before the blunt scissors were wielded, but it was difficult to make any worthwhile assessment of *The Leopard* until two decades had passed and the original version was re-released in 1983.

From the opening moments, as the camera sweeps majestically through a pair of high iron gates and across gardens surrounding the Prince of Salina's palace, a powerful feeling of 'place' is imposed upon the audience. This is no mere movie location chosen because it looks as if it could be right – it *is* the place. The crumbling grandeur of the palace, the colour of its stonework matching the dry, burnt hills in which it stands, is an integral part of the landscape.

It appears as though the palace has been standing there as long as the land has been there, and will remain for ever, but then, as the aristocratic family are seen at Sunday morning prayers, the first discordant note is heard. Running as muted counterpoint to the intoning of the word of God is an excited clamour from the world outside. Some members of the family look towards the window, others to the door; one son of the house moves to leave but, without discernible movement, the kneeling Don Fabrizio, Prince of Salina (Lancaster) forbids such action and thus stamps his authority upon this gathering.

Prayers over, the cause of the disturbance is discovered. The servants have found the dead body of a soldier in the palace grounds. The distant war, the conflict between the Bourbon state and the red-shirted followers of Garibaldi, has touched this quiet corner of Sicily and nothing will ever be the same again. Or will it?

Now that the Garibaldini have landed on the island, loyalties need to be focused and Sicilians must take sides. The Prince's nephew, Tancredi (Alain Delon), chooses to join the Red Shirts but the manner of his decision and the casually flamboyant way he leaves to join the revolutionaries betray his lack of ideological commitment. To Tancredi it is all a game, a sport in which he hunts men not animals. The paucity of the prevalent ideology is emphasized by the fact that the only difference between hunter and hunted is the way in which they dress. Language, nationality, background; all these are the same.

The Prince does not attempt to deter his favourite nephew, a man he regards more as a son (and a favourite son at that) from his whim.

The Prince of Salina is a man of vision yet has no illusions; he knows his future better than anyone. The Bourbons are finished and if the aristocracy is to endure then it must accommodate the revolutionaries within its crumbling walls.

He is also completely in tune with his homeland. In a beautifully realized scene with the family priest, Father Pirrone (Romolo Valli), these two representatives of sacred and secular Sicily discuss the Prince's carnal appetite, unslaked by his dry marriage to Maria Stella (Rina Morelli). They also muse upon the past, the future and the war, but it is Don Fabrizio who has the

most far-sighted view beside which the Church is positively
myopic.

This difference in the breadth and scope of vision is
demonstrated by three telescopes standing in the Prince's
study, each pointed skywards. As the Prince stands at the
window, gazing out over the parched hills of his beloved land,
he draws the view to the attention of the priest. Father Pirrone
moves towards the window, glances incuriously outside, then
gives all his attention to cleaning a smudge of dirt from the
barrel of one of the telescopes. As the Prince continues to speak,
the priest moves away, returning to the desk and his studies, his
back towards the window. The Church may hold the souls of
the Sicilians, but it understands them no more than it
understood the primitive races of Africa and Asia which it
brought into its bosom with scant regard for the here and now,
despite its professed concern for the hereafter.

Later, when it is time for the Prince and his family to take their
annual holiday at their summer palace in Donnafugata, the
fighting has abated. Garibaldi has returned to the mainland and
an uneasy peace reigns. Tancredi has rejoined the family, the
only memory of the fighting is a bandage which covers an
injured eye and which he wears with piratical insouciance. For
him the war has really been just another sporting adventure. But
Tancredi has not entirely abandoned the military life; he is now
an officer in the regular army and owes allegiance to King Victor
Emmanuel, a Savoyard to whom Garibaldi has also turned.

Along the way to Donnafugata, the first clear intimations of
the prevalence of the old order become apparent. A barricade
thrown across the road and manned by soldiers, who were
themselves former Red Shirts, is contemptuously ordered aside
by Tancredi so that Don Fabrizio's carriage can pass
unhindered.

When the Prince's entourage reaches Donnafugata any
lingering doubts that the revolution has changed anything are
cast aside in a dozen ways, both obvious and discreet.

The town band, drawn up to greet the Prince with a rousing
tune, stands proudly in the town square. Behind the musicians,
ignored now as they venerate the old aristocracy, is a wall upon
which is daubed the slogan: Viva Garibaldi.

But there have been some changes, even if they have not been

made by the Garibaldini, and they do not escape Don Fabrizio's
notice as he greets the townspeople. Some are in his employ,
others live in Donnafugata and are slowly achieving a new kind
of power. Representative of the former is Don Ciccio Tumeo
(Serge Reggiani), the Prince's huntsman, who is a shy, failed
composer. The latter group is represented by the town's mayor,
Don Calogero Sedara (Paolo Stoppa), a man whose landholdings threaten to outstrip the Prince's, but who desperately
wants to be accepted as a social equal of the aristocracy.

During the family's stay in Donnafugata, past and present are
drawn closer and the first intimations of what the future holds
appear. Don Calogero has a beautiful daughter, Angelica
(Claudia Cardinale), and when the Prince observes the
immediate and obvious physical attraction displayed by
Angelica and Tancredi he resolves that they shall marry. The
fact that his own daughter, Concetta (Lucilla Morlacchi), is in
love with Tancredi is brusquely set aside. If it is to survive the
aristocracy needs new blood in both its geneaology and its
financial veins.

Curious to know the background of the family into which he
is preparing to marry his nephew, the Prince talks to Don Ciccio
when they are out hunting. According to his huntsman,
Angelica's mother (whom no one in the village but he has ever
seen) is extraordinarily beautiful, but as earthy as her primitive
hill-dwelling forebears. This reassures the Prince; rejuvenation
of his family seems certain if a woman with such fecund
antecedents marries the virile Tancredi.

Ciccio and the Prince also debate their differing political
views. In a recent referendum in Donnafugata, Don Ciccio
voted against the new order, preferring instead to stand by the
old order represented by the Prince. The Prince himself,
ever-conscious of the need to accept the inevitable, has voted in
favour of change.

This scene between the Don Fabrizio, Prince of Salina, and his
huntsman, in which the outpouring of tangled political
philosophy from Don Ciccio is counterpointed by monosyllabic
but patently realistic interventions from the Prince, all played
out on a hillside with a backdrop formed by the stark landscape,
is among the most powerful in the film.

Contrasting with the closeness displayed between the Prince

and his employee is the uneasiness with which he approaches Don Calogero. In the scene in which the Prince asks that Angelica and Tancredi be allowed to marry, he does not want to make the physical contact necessary to seal the bargain. Tradition requires him to embrace and kiss the father of the bride-to-be. When he does finally overcome his reluctance, he contrives to simultaneously accede to tradition and underline their true positions in the scheme of things. The Prince lifts the mayor off the ground as he makes the gesture; Don Calogero might have the new power and the new money, but he still needs the support of the aristocracy whose status in society will always be beyond his reach.

Later, when Chevally (Leslie French), a representative of the new government, comes over from the mainland to seek the Prince's participation, Don Fabrizio acknowledges the reality of Don Calogero's position. Refusing to take a seat in the upper house of the Senate, the wryly comments that he lacks the self-deception necessary for a man who wants to guide others. He then puts forward Don Calogero as an alternative. Whatever his social background, the reality is that Don Calogero is the new power in the land. The Prince also acknowledges that there may even be a new aristocracy of sorts. In a dry reference to Don Calogero Sedara's vain attempts to fabricate a family tree which bears links to some long-dead nobleman, the Prince points out that Sedara will soon be an ancient name.

As Chevally leaves the island, the Prince reflects upon another aspect of their conversation together: the persisting theme of the film that all change is designed to ensure that there will be no change. He and his kind are the lions and the leopards, the others are jackals and hyenas. The leopards might one day be replaced by the jackals but in the end the natural balance will remain the same.

The final forty-five minutes of the film take place at a grand ball given by another member of Sicily's nobility. To this extravagant function come all the members of the island's ruling class. They are joined by a handful of the parvenus, including Don Calogero Sedara and his daughter, Angelica, who is now betrothed to the Prince's nephew, Tancredi. A handful of officers of the new army are also there. They have recently captured four of the Garibaldini who still retain revolutionary ideals which sit uncomfortably in this post-revolutionary compromise. Come the dawn, the four men are to be shown the error of their ways.

The totality of the ballroom scene is quite breathtaking in its attention to sumptuous detail. The squalor of the streets outside does not penetrate here; there is only richness. The vivid colours of gowns and uniforms, the tapestries and flowers, even the food and wine, all glow with vibrant life.

As he strolls through this pageant of all that money and power can buy, the Prince grows slowly disaffected by it all. The stark contrast between this setting and the burnt-out landscapes he has so admired throughout the preceding scenes underline the dichotomy which exists within him. He is no longer at ease with his own kind, yet he cannot be a part of the new order. He is a man out of time.

Feeling suddenly unwell, the Prince enters the library of the palace in which the ball is being held. On one wall hangs an oil painting of a deathbed scene: an ageing patriarch lies dying while his family gather around his bed.

Angelica and Tancredi find the Prince here and the girl expresses her happiness and her thanks that he has helped bring about the forthcoming marriage. She kisses him and asks him to dance with her. Aware of the sudden jealousy of his nephew, the Prince demurs but is persuaded.

The Prince and Angelica enter the ballroom and as they waltz the floor becomes theirs alone – everyone else stands and watches. Tancredi's jealousy is matched by that of the Prince's wife, Princess Maria Stella (Rina Morelli), but neither has any real cause to be so disturbed. The underlying and carefully underplayed attraction between these two people, the ageing aristocrat and the exotic young plebeian beauty, cannot go further than this public waltz.

The dancing over, the Prince is more than ever aware of his own mortality. His life is almost over, the vitality and virility which once flowed through him is drying up more rapidly than the land he loves so much. The moments he has just spent in close proximity to Angelica have awakened memories of his lost youth, echoes of his fading sexual prowess. His unexpected tears are not self-pitying, they are tangible evidence of another, perhaps final, stage in the development of his self-knowledge.

Resigned now, the Prince decides to walk home, leaving Tancredi to accompany the Princess and the rest of the family. He has silently abdicated his role as patriarch.

Outside it is dawn, a priest hurries by and the Prince kneels to pray. The carriages carrying his family drive homewards and the occupants are suddenly disturbed by a volley of rifle fire as the four recalcitrant Garibaldini are executed.

Completely alone now, Don Fabrizio, Prince of Salina, walks slowly through the deserted streets of the town. A new day is dawning and with it a new society is born, but it is one in which he will have no part to play.

Technically, *The Leopard* cannot be faulted. Now restored to its original format and colour (Fox had used CinemaScope and De Luxe Colour on the print released in 1963), the beauty of Giuseppe Rotunno's photography is revealed. Not until 1974, when Gordon Willis photographed similar landscapes for *The Godfather II* would a comparable feel for the texture of dry Mediterranean hills and buildings appear on cinema screens. The interiors, especially those in the Prince's palace and the ballroom of the closing sequence, however different, are similarly perfect demonstrations of the cinematographer's art.

Visconti's direction is in effortless control. There may have been lavishness on the set (the film cost £2.5 million in the days when that was a great deal of film-making money) but not a penny of it was wasted. Everything, every tiny gesture, every apparently insignificant artefact, takes on meaning and adds to the resonance, the feel, even the smell of the finished product.

The director's despair at the treatment of his work by the butchers who edited and reprocessed *The Leopard* before its 1963 general release can be fully understood now that the film is restored to its former glory. It is a sad reflection on the state of film as industry, rather than film as art, that *The Leopard* should have been treated in this way. It is almost as if a team of merchants had painted over sections of the ceiling of the Sistine Chapel because it didn't fit their image of what a work of art should be.

There are no weak acting performances in *The Leopard*. Every role, down to the smallest of the bit-part players is thoroughly conceived, visually accurate, and excellently portrayed. The larger of the supporting roles are all finely executed with special reference due to Paolo Stoppa, Serge Reggiani (as the Prince's huntsman), and Romolo Valli (as the family priest).

Claudia Cardinale's interpretation of the earthy and sensuous Angelica is exactly the right combination of bawdiness and beauty. Perhaps she is a shade too confident in her first steps among the upper classes, but maybe a real Angelica would similarly have lacked ambition. Alain Delon invests the dashing Tancredi with an ideal blend of verve and intensity, never quite concealing the undercurrent of arrogance his station in life has brought him.

As Don Fabrizio, Prince of Salina, Burt Lancaster becomes the character more completely than he had achieved with any of his roles before this time. Visconti had wanted Laurence Olivier for the part and when he proved unavailable was affronted when producer Goffredo Lombardo suggested Lancaster after he had seen him in *Judgement at Nuremberg*. It is fortunate that chance brought Visconti and Lancaster together. The actor's calm control of every situation in which he finds himself, the magnetic power he brings to every scene in which he plays (and he is on screen for the greater part of the film) leads inescapably to the conclusion that this was a role for which he was made.

Despite the atrocious editing and dubbing of the 1963 release, Lancaster came in for high praise in some quarters. Peter Baker, in *Films and Filming* (December 1963) remarked on 'a splendid performance [which] gets behind the character as though he knows and loves every subtlety of Lampedusa's writing.' In *Sight & Sound* (Winter 1963/4) David Robinson wrote that 'Burt Lancaster has quite confounded all expectation by embodying the noble Prince of Salina, whose liberalism is half policy and half the indolence of an exhausted race.'

When *The Leopard* was re-released in its restored version in 1983 Alexander Walker wrote in the London *Evening Standard* that 'Lancaster can, in a word, *impose* himself. It takes some doing to dominate the most lavish and sensual set-pieces of social ostentation ever seen on the screen.'

Lancaster was now in full command of his capabilities and was able and ready to tackle any role. Inevitably, whatever followed immediately after *The Leopard* would be something of an anticlimax for him. For audiences of the day, however, it didn't seem a hard act to follow because the hacked version of the film was not then recognized as a masterpiece.

In the event, there was nothing inadequate about either of the two films which followed, both of which were directed by John Frankenheimer.

Seven Days in May (1964) was the first of what became for Lancaster a steady stream of appearances in the uniform of a senior army officer.

The story concerns Colonel Martin 'Jiggs' Casey (Kirk Douglas) who discovers that his right-wing superior, General James M. Scott (Lancaster), is planning a military coup to wrest power from the President of the United States whose policies he sees as a threat to national security. President Jordan Lyman (Fredric March) has recently gone out on a limb and opposed his military chiefs of staff by signing a treaty with the Russians intended to diminish the threat of nuclear holocaust. Scott believes the president's pacifist behaviour to be an act of treason and he takes secret action to arrest what he sees as a slide into subordination to the Soviets.

Little by little, a disbelieving Colonel Casey picks up seemingly unrelated but collectively disturbing facts. Among these is the existence of a secret army base in the middle of the Texas nowhereland, a base known only to the military high command. Coded messages are constantly passing between General Scott and other senior officers who meet secretly at night. Casey eventually decides that Scott is planning a coup for an upcoming weekend when military exercises are scheduled. As a part of these exercises the president is to be isolated, and Scott will take advantage of this to stage his uprising.

Casey tells the president of his suspicions and findings. The president promptly alerts some of the few men he can trust, one of whom is Senator Raymond Clark (Edmond O'Brien), an alcoholic, who travels south and gains access to the Texas base, but is held there against his will. Meanwhile, the president sends another trusted aide, Paul Girard (Martin Balsam), to the Mediterranean to confront Admiral Barnswell (John Houseman) whom Casey knows to have so far avoided total commitment to Scott's conspiracy. The admiral makes a written statement which he hands to Girard, but the presidential aide's return flight crashes and Girard is killed.

On a more mundane level, Casey has been investigating

Eleanor Holbrook (Ava Gardner), a former mistress of General Scott, who holds some damaging letters. Despite the danger of his situation, the president refuses to use these letters and instead makes a public demand for the resignation of his chiefs of staff.

One by one, then in a disconcerting rush, Scott's fellow conspirators desert his cause, but the maverick general still clings to a faint hope that he can carry the day alone. Then word comes that Admiral Barnswell's statement has been found in the wreckage of the crash which ended Paul Girard's life.

With no support and his own credibility destroyed, General James Scott accepts his defeat but can accept neither the weakness of his colleagues nor what he regards as his betrayal by his subordinate, Colonel Casey.

With its careful attention to detail, especially in the military command's Washington bunker, and visually splendid scenes such as those set in the Texas wasteland, where Senator Clark's car is stopped by a helicopter patrol, the film is always worth watching.

Among the strongest moments is the manner in which Senator Clark's alcoholism is used to destroy his support for the president. Unlike many such characterizations in films, Clark is no closet drinker; everyone knows his weakness, thus allowing the opposition to use it against him. When he is locked in a small and stiflingly hot room with the only liquid a bottle of his favourite booze, the scene's tension builds inexorably as the senator sweats out his addiction.

Allowing the audience to learn what is really happening only as Casey and the president's men discover the meaning of all the cryptic odds and ends that bewilder them, Frankenheimer sustains suspense and a surprising level of credibility. Indeed, as time passed, the prospect displayed in *Seven Days in May* became disturbingly more probable than when the film was first made. Even if recent rapprochement between America and Russia and the breakup of the Warsaw Pact make the basic premise improbable, the paranoia of right-wing reactionaries in America will readily find another enemy under the national bed; when the Democrats eventually get their act back together and a more liberal president occupies the Oval Office, who can tell what might happen?

The acting in *Seven Days in May* is solid, with Douglas holding in the hysteria which marred several of his roles of the period. March is excellent as the harrassed conscientious president and there is good support from Balsam, Houseman and George Macready. The best performance of all comes from O'Brien as the alcoholic senator whose weakness threatens attempts to expose the conspirators. O'Brien was unsuccessfully nominated for an Oscar.

By now turned 50, Lancaster looked the part of the general (and although a little bulkier had lost none of the panther grace with which he moved), but he had the disadvantage of being absent from the film's best scenes.

Another kind of military setting provided the basis for the second in this pair of Lancaster-Frankenheimer collaborations. Set in wartime France, *The Train* (1964) is an interesting and often exciting thriller which uses real events for its storyline (and is the film on which the star was working when he flew to Washington to make his stand known on the Civil Rights issue).

A German colonel, von Waldheim (Paul Scofield), has gathered together a priceless collection of French Impressionist paintings looted from Paris museums and galleries. He is trying to get the collection back to Germany by train but French Resistance leader Labiche (Lancaster) is determined to stop him.

By giving the two principals untypical characteristics, the story of their duel gains immeasurably from what could have been just another chase-movie. Von Waldheim is not mindlessly serving a master; he wants the paintings for himself because 'beauty belongs to the man who can appreciate it'. Labiche is not aesthetically concerned with the art works von Waldheim has stolen, he just wants to stop the German getting away with anything. His grim resolve would not have weakened had the train been filled with cabbages.

Labiche is obsessed and so too is his adversary and it is this confrontation between obsessives that gives *The Train* a dimension which lifts it above the more popular and better-remembered *Von Ryan's Express* (1965). Looked at solely for its nuts-and-bolts expertise, the later film has more dash and verve, but *The Train* provides a better understanding of men at war with one another and with themselves.

There is also a more realistic appraisal of the politics of war.

Throughout, Labiche is properly cynical at the political machinations attendant upon the successes of the advancing allied armies. He knows that delays to allow the French to enter Paris at the head of the triumphant liberators may look well in newspapers and history books, but what of the men who will die while politicians wrangle?

The main characters are played with great conviction. Paul Scofield stands out in what was only his third screen role. Although essentially a stage player, Scofield's fine talent should have been persuaded more often into films. Introspective and subtle, conveying more with a movement of an eye than many men can convey with entire body and voice, Scofield has much in common with Lancaster in his more internalized roles. The nature of *The Train* is such that they are not allowed to play good scenes together and thus the realms of what might have been had to wait until, fortunately, they worked together again.

Lancaster's portrayal of the wearily cynical yet grimly determined Resistance fighter is a fine example of his ability to give depth and purpose to an outwardly physical character.

Although perhaps not apparent to most filmgoers, his role as a man who cares nothing for art takes on added texture when the actor's own interests are considered. Among the paintings he has collected over the years are works by Renoir, Utrillo and Chagall.

With the 1960s half over, Lancaster's career was at a high point. Commercially and artistically, he was achieving all that his ambitious nature could want. Yet he showed no signs of tiring.

Before the decade was out, his continuing enthusiasm for work would lead him into even more commercial successes as he made frequent explorations into the American West; and into a role which proved to be a commercial disaster, only to take on the status of a cult movie in later years.

His continuing addiction to work was also to have its effect upon his private life when Norma, who had tolerated this and his eye for pretty co-stars with outward equanimity, decided that enough was enough.

6 Dreams and Nightmares

In his early fifties but looking a good ten years younger, Burt Lancaster was still more than capable of playing romantic leads. But, by the mid-1960s he was displaying a marked tendency to portray older men and was still keen to explore areas of film-making outside the usual commercial run.

However, bills had to be paid, commitments fulfilled, responsibilities met, and he accomplished all these needs with a string of three westerns none of which was outstanding – although only the first proved to be something of a dud.

This was *The Hallelujah Trail* (1965), a rather sorry affair, overlong by at least a third and never measuring up to its on-paper promise.

The confused story (helped out by maps and commentary for the slower members of the audience) centres upon a wagonload of whisky almost everyone wants. The Indians want it; the law wants it; parched but otherwise upright citizens want it. And a bunch of temperance crusaders under the reluctant protection of the US Cavalry commanded by Colonel Thadeus Gearhart (Lancaster) want it. But they intend to destroy it so that no one else can have it.

It all gets very muddled and while deliberate complications can add spice to a film, here the confusions are merely confusing.

Long before the end, the audience and most of the cast lost interest in what happened to the hooch. Actually, Cora Templeton Massingale (Lee Remick), the leading light of the temperance movement, dumps it into a quicksand.

Much more lively and exciting was *The Professionals* (1966), which follows the fortunes of four men hired by railroad magnate J.W. Grant (Ralph Bellamy) to rescue his wife Maria

(Claudia Cardinale) who has been kidnapped by bandit leader Jesus Raza (Jack Palance).

The men Grant hires are all tough professionals: Bill Dolworth (Lancaster) is a demolition expert, Jake Sharp (Woody Strode) is a tracker who can also use a longbow when silent long-range killing is needed, Hans Ehrengard (Robert Ryan) has a fine hand with horses, creatures he loves considerably more than he loves his fellow men. The leader of the group is Enrico Fardan (Lee Marvin), a whizz with firearms, especially the new-fangled machine-gun.

The quartet sets out in pursuit of the beautiful Maria and her captor, intent on carrying out the task for which they've been hired, while carefully ignoring the morality of their situation which pits them against revolutionaries with whom they once shared ideals.

Try as they will, questions of morality surface and the hired professionals discover that their detachment is more easily undermined than they imagined. Maria is not the helpless victim of an evil bandit. She was forced into marriage with J.W. Grant when she really wanted to be with Raza, her true love. Maria has gone willingly to Mexico with Raza and is party to the ransom he is demanding for her 'return', knowing how he needs the money for the revolution.

The four Americans are thus faced with a series of moral decisions: do they take on and fight (and probably kill) men whose dreams were once theirs; do they drag an unwilling woman from the arms of the man she loves and return her to the man who merely 'owns' her; do they submerge ideals and morals in order to carry out the task to which they are bound by money?

This complex undertow makes the story infinitely more interesting than a routine western. Nevertheless, on the surface it is tough and exciting and has enough gripping action to satisfy the most saddlesore front-row cowboy.

In the end, despite having spent long and dangerous hours in transporting Maria and capturing Raza, the professionals decide to forget the money and free their captives. This last-minute turnabout fits the characters of the four as they have developed throughout the film and makes a satisfying if slightly unlikely ending.

Produced, directed and written by Richard Brooks, *The Professionals* is above-average western fare. Taken only at surface level it has many good moments and the set pieces are well staged. When the moral principles which lurk beneath the story's surface are examined, the film's more elementary qualities are enhanced. Even the participation of the Mexicans is adult and sympathetic, especially so in the light of the fact that only too often Mexicans have replaced Indians as all-purpose biters of Hollywood dust.

The casual manner in which Tinseltown's film-makers have maligned minorities might well have contributed to the all-pervading lack of understanding with which the not-so-silent majority looks upon their less-fortunate fellows. In the case of the Mexicans this might well prove to have been a tactical error as the number of Spanish Americans resident in Southern California increases. Not only do they now have considerable if unaligned political muscle, they also have potential financial influence even if only on the simplistic level of which movies they will pay to see.

Latter-day film-makers might well take their cue from the manner in which their future audience should be treated from *The Professionals*, even if the tale's leading Mexican is played by a non-Mexican.

Nevertheless, and naturally enough given the form and structure of the film, the four professionals are given maximum screentime and the actors concerned all deliver sound performances.

Robert Ryan never set a foot wrong in any film he made and although quiet and sick (in real life at the time as well as in character), he is exceptionally sure-footed here. Lee Marvin's career was dogged by the fact that all too often he was called upon to play roles which reflected what audiences imagined to be extensions of his real-life persona. For much of the first half of this film his is the principal character and he sustains the task effortlessly, obviously enjoying a role with depth and as always on such occasions producing a fine performance.

Woody Strode is another actor who was never less than good when allowed a role that did not demean him as a man. Unfortunately, this rarely happened because Hollywood has usually proved to be hopelessly inept, if not downright offensive, in its treatment of black actors. Unable – or at least unwilling – to grant on-screen blacks roles much above the menial level on which real-life blacks were employed in the studios (unless they could sing or dance), the result was a succession of tasteless embarrassments. So ingrained did the subservient role of blacks on-screen become that when black became box-office and black hands held some of the off-screen reins there was often little to distinguish the new from the old. Stereotyping remained and blacks still behaved in the way expected of them by ill-educated white audiences.

Woody Strode did at least manage to find one role in his career which largely overcame the stereotyping: the title role in John Ford's patchy but well-intentioned *Sergeant Rutledge* (1960).

Burt Lancaster's role in *The Professionals* contains many intriguing facets displaying the problems of a man who is simultaneously of his time and yet out of it. A man hung between conflicting senses of duty: to himself, to his comrades-in-arms, to his employer, to his past, and to his long-buried ideals. It is a measure of Lancaster's ability that all these conflicts are satisfactorily realized. From half-way through the film, when he takes over from Marvin as the central character, he stamps his screen authority on the film. As always in action films he moves well and gracefully – or with as much grace as any man could muster when made to trot around clad in long-johns for much of his screentime.

The Professionals is a thoroughly enjoyable piece of film-making and, as befits a film with such a title, it is all highly professional. The fans loved it, but it didn't please everyone. Pauline Kael, writing in the *New Yorker*, bleakly dismissed it as having 'the expertise of a cold old whore with practised hands and no thoughts of love.'

The third of Lancaster's short string of westerns was a similarly professional job and this time even had a cold old whore among the cast of characters.

The Scalphunters (1968) tells of a surly, ill-tempered trapper named Joe Bass (Lancaster) who happens upon a gang of bounty hunters as they slaughter a band of harmless Indians for their scalps, worth money from a government tacitly engaged in genocide.

Diverted from their grisly task, the bounty hunters, led by Jim

Howie (Telly Savalas), steal Joe Bass's skins, the results of many months' solitary and arduous work. Prompted more by this personal affront than by the killings he has witnessed, Joe sets out to recover his skins and is joined in this task by Joseph Winfield Lee (Ossie Davis), a runaway slave.

Despite the opening slaughter of peaceful Indians, *The Scalphunters* is played for laughs rather than thrills, but there is simultaneously a degree of serious attention to man's ability to live off other men and even to accept wholesale murder just so long as he isn't killed and someone else does the killing.

Clichés are generally avoided. The illiterate, slovenly trapper and the highly educated upright slave dislike one another and constantly engage in verbal conflict, each aiming many of his barbs at the other's colour. The contrasts in their literacy and the disparities in their intellectual capacity are given a twist: the black man is smartest, but the white trapper is most at one with nature.

The principals play well in roles that have more depth and subtlety than the film's synopsis might imply. Especially good is Shelley Winters who portrays Kate, Howie's mistress, an overweight and over-the-hill whore, with considerable panache. She also contrives to bring to her scenes qualities perhaps barely imagined by the scriptwriter. For example, when a tribe of Indians finally overcome the bounty hunters, she accepts her fate with equanimity declaring that the Indian chief is going to get 'the damnedest white squaw in the [entire] Kiowa nation.' She also delivers a line that is funny, faintly shocking, and infinitely sad: 'What the hell, they're only men.'

As with other black actors, Ossie Davis seldom gains the parts his talents richly deserve. There are exceptions as with *Gone Are the Days!* (1963), which was based upon his own stage play, *Purlie Victorious*, in which he has roles into which he can sink himself. In *The Scalphunters* he comes off rather well, mainly because of his role's carefully avoided potential for stereotyping, and this is one of his best films.

The slave is no simple-minded lunk, but neither is he a selfless hero riding to the rescue of his white partner. Instead, he is out to save his own skin which is in jeopardy because of its colour. He never loses sight of this fact and neither does he allow his white partner to ignore it.

The outcome of the toe-to-toe scrap he has with Lancaster would never have been contemplated in earlier times. In a less well-realized film the white man would have won; in most of the well-intentioned but artificially liberal films of the 1960s the black man would have been the victor. Here, nobody wins, white and black come out hurt but equal. It isn't a cop-out ending, it's the way such an encounter would probably have ended.

As the grizzled unkempt mountain man Lancaster makes no attempt to look young; indeed he plays the part as if older, foretelling the westerns he would make in the next decade when age would bring an added dimension to his portrayals.

Lancaster's role in his next film was in sharp contrast to that of the slovenly Joe Bass. Neither could the setting and ambience be much further removed from the rough and tumble of the Old West.

Uncompromisingly contemporary, *The Swimmer* (1968) is located in the all-too-real America of broken promises and forgotten dreams. It is also a hugely uncommercial film which failed at the box office and was badly mauled by critics, but which has climbed steadily in status over the years until it has become a cult and can now be seen as pungent commentary on the state of the nation and one of its star's best roles.

The Swimmer begins when Ned Merrill (Lancaster), clad only in swimming-trunks, appears in the garden of a luxury house. Languidly sipping cocktils around a swimming-pool sits a group of overtly wealthy people. Clearly, they all know Ned and express both surprise and pleasure at seeing him after a long absence.

Ned, physically in great shape, is out of place among the overweight and overdressed, and although he seems outwardly at ease there is the subtlest of hints that something isn't quite right. He takes a drink with his friends and when asked about his family, detachedly answers, 'Lucinda's just fine, and the girls are at home playing tennis.'

Looking out across the trees that fill the valley below (the film was shot in Fairfield County, Connecticut) Merrill remarks that visible among the trees are swimming-pools in gardens of other houses, the homes of more of his friends. He decides that he will swim home, using the pools as a pathway to his own house and family.

But, as Merrill reaches the next house and takes his ritualistic swim in another pool, hints emerge that all is not quite what it seems. This time, the greetings from the owners are strained and subtle tensions flicker beneath the surface.

As he progresses, old antagonisms arise: one woman believes that Merrill caused the death of a loved one, his daughters are vilified for the way they live their lives, another woman reveals that she was his mistress, and there are hints that he is bankrupt.

During this strange personal odyssey, Ned Merrill begins to discover himself. Apparently without memory of his past, he learns that although he was once a part of this wealthy and exclusive social set he has somehow grown away from them, but he knows neither how nor why.

At each stop along the way, when questioned about his family, he repeats the same answer, 'Lucinda's just fine, and the girls are at home playing tennis', and with each repetition it becomes less certain that this is the truth.

Merrill encounters a young girl he knew when she was a child and for a while she accompanies him, but through a misunderstanding he alienates her, just as he has clearly alienated everyone from his past.

Then he injures his foot and is transformed from a lithe athlete into a limping, awkwardly ordinary man.

It isn't only the swimmer who changes; steadily, the luxury of the homes and gardens and pools through which he passes become more obviously artificial. Everywhere are gross plastic and chrome appendages, blatant displays of wealth and status.

Eventually, Merrill reaches the main highway which he has to cross to enter the last pool of his journey. But this is not a private luxury pool. This is the civic swimming-pool and for the first time he will not have the water to himself for it is filled with a shouting, seething mass of humanity. Swimming is virtually impossible for anyone but, in the event, Merrill is refused admission. He has no money and his foot is bleeding.

Worse for the increasingly disturbed Merrill, some of the people in the pool are openly antagonistic. These are not former friends prepared to conceal past conflicts beneath unctuous pleasantries; these are angry acquaintances who harangue him for his past behaviour.

The denizens of the luxury homes he has passed through, the owners of those clean, unoccupied swimming-pools, shallow and sycophantic and palpably insincere as they are, represented success. They have attained the American Dream. The heaving, angry mass in the municipal pool are failures when measured by this society's standards. For them, the American Dream is a nightmare.

As Ned Merrill leaves the crowded pool and approaches his own home, the sky clouds over and rain begins to fall. Hesitantly, for he is no longer certain what he will find, he enters his own garden. It is overgrown; no daughters play on the weed-covered tennis court. The pool is empty.

As the rain becomes a torrent he reaches his front door but finds it locked. The house is shuttered, deserted, and has obviously been that way for years. He beats on the door but no one opens it because no one is there. In tears, he slumps to the ground. The swimmer's journey is over; he has rediscovered his past and it is empty.

It is in its treatment of the questions raised and the answers suggested that the film's greatest strengths lie. Indeed, there are no real answers, merely loose ends examined and left. Have Lucinda and the girls left Merrill, or did he leave them? Are they alive or dead? Did he leave his luxurious environment voluntarily or was he pushed; has he been in prison; has he suffered a mental breakdown?

We never know for sure because we do not really need to know.

As for the swimmer's emotional state; whatever brief encounter he might have had with normality during his aquatic odyssey, he ends in utter despair. Like the clamouring mob in the municipal pool, he is one of life's losers. Unlike them, he did, however fleetingly, touch the American Dream and found it wanting.

Not surprisingly, thanks to its bold questioning of much that motivates American society, *The Swimmer* failed to become a commercial success in the United States. It also failed in Britain and elsewhere because its allegorical nature depends too much upon an understanding of an alien society, its mores and standards. A few years on, as America faced up to Watergate and, briefly, made an honest attempt to acknowledge the nation's cancerous structure, the film might have had a more generous reception. Certainly, as time has passed, *The Swimmer*'s trenchant examination of contemporary society has found growing support and, alone among the star's films, it has gained cult status.

The screenplay by Eleanor Perry is skilfully directed by Frank Perry (one sequence was reshot in California by Sydney Pollack) and David Quaid's photography brilliantly evokes the shifting mood of the film.

All the supporting roles are played well, although the linear structure of the plot doesn't allow anyone much screentime before the swimmer moves on to his next stage of rediscovery.

Lancaster is excellent, his internal brooding undergoing subtle shifts as he discovers a little more about himself only to find that one question has been replaced by another.

Only a handful of critics liked the film when it was first released and Vincent Canby, writing in the *New York Times*, expressed some of the ambivalence felt by many when he stated, 'I like Burt Lancaster, who is essentially miscast in the title role, for having wanted to do it. Without his interest the film would probably never have been made ... As do few movies, *The Swimmer* stays in the memory like an echo that never quite disappears.'

Lancaster's interest in this film – more of a commitment really – is underlined by the fact that he trained for three months, determined that his fear of water would not inhibit his performance.

In September 1968 Lancaster had a minor brush with the law and used it – or so he later claimed – to enhance his understanding of one particular aspect of American society.

Stopped for exceeding the 45 mph speed limit along Pacific Coast Highway at Malibu, he declined to sign the police-officer's ticket (which calls only for a promise to appear in court). Told that the alternative was a night in jail he stuck to his decision. Deputy Mason Dixon (yes, really) later stated that his star guest 'had sufficient money to bail out but he said something about wanting to get an education and there's no time like now. He just decided to stay in jail.'

Next day, presumably better educated if not rested, Lancaster handed over $65 and bailed himself out.

Whatever benefits he drew from a few hours in the Malibu lock-up were not of much use to him in his next film although, on reflection, it might have been better if he'd stayed in jail.

William Eastlake's novel upon which *Castle Keep* (1969) is based is far from being a straightforward war story. Although it is certainly that, it is simultaneously a fantasy, an allegory, and a dissertation upon the human condition. This floating, ambiguous approach to the subject-matter created massive problems for screenwriter and director which are never satisfactorily resolved.

During World War II a detachment of soldiers under the command of war-weary Major Falconer (Lancaster) is detailed to defend a Belgian castle against overwhelming odds. The castle is stuffed with art treasures which the owner, Count de Maldorais (Jean-Pierre Aumont) desperately wants to save from destruction. The count is also eager that his wife, Thérèse (Astrid Heeren), should become pregnant thus allowing the noble line to continue but as he cannot father a child he encourages the major to take her to bed.

The count's artistic obsession is supported by one of Falconer's men, Captain Beckman (Patrick O'Neal), an art historian in civilian life.

Beckman is not alone in having a private and non-belligerent interest that takes precedence over his military duties. Private Benjamin (Al Freeman Jr) is writing the great war novel; Lieutenant Amberjack (Tony Bill), destined for the church, is desperately eager to sample the fleshly pleasures of the local whorehouse. This establishment is also frequented with much less soul-searching and considerably more success than the putative priest by Sergeant DeVaca (Michael Conrad) and Elk (James Patterson), a Native American.

Two other members of Falconer's motley band are in love. Sergeant Rossi (Peter Falk), a baker back home, dallies with the widow of the local breadmaker and dreams of setting up in business with her. As for Corporal Clearboy (Scott Wilson), he is in love with a Volkswagen automobile and dreams of heaven knows what.

And drifting around the periphery of Falconer's confused unit is a growing batch of American soldiers bearing a white flag and desperately anxious to give up what they believe to be a senseless struggle.

When the Germans finally attack the castle, Falconer needs all his powers of persuasion to bring his men out of their various deluded dreams and back into the reality of the brutal and bloody war – a reality which, for Falconer and most of them, means death. When the smoke and dust has settled only Private Benjamin and the countess have survived.

Good intentions abound throughout *Castle Keep*, but ultimately go largely unrealized. The chief fault for the unsatisfactory nature of the film lies in the woolly adaptation of the book, although Sydney Pollack's direction is often more in keeping with the surface war story than with the underlying and much more fragile fantasy. (Lancaster had quarrelled with Pollack during the making of *The Scalphunters* but wanted to work with him again because he was 'the man who really worked me the hardest, and the man I best communicated with.')

The acting performances are variable with most praise going, rightly, to Falk, Freeman and Wilson. Set against good performances like these in what are, in many cases, somewhat eccentric and much larger-than-life roles, Lancaster's portrayal of the one-eyed company commander is competent but uninspired.

Critics were not kind. Paul Warshow, writing in *Film Quarterly* (Summer 1970), was typical in his dismissal of the film's pretentions declaring that *Castle Keep* was 'an artificial, forced allegory which could never decide whether it was operating from a realistic base or from one of abstract poetic myth. On either level the film was awful ... and the shift back and forth between the two levels was excruciating.'

Lancaster's next film also hinted at more than eventually reached the screen, although in this case the end result was more coherent and better to look at.

The eponymous heroes of *The Gypsy Moths* (1969) are a trio of aerial stuntmen who arrive at the small Kansas town of Bridgeville where they are to perform during Independence Day celebrations. The youngest of the trio is Malcolm Webson (Scott Wilson) who once lived in Bridgeville, and he takes his companions, Joe Browdy and Mike Rettig (Gene Hackman and Lancaster) to visit his aunt and uncle.

Rettig dislikes the claustrophobic lifestyle of Elizabeth and

John Brandon (Deborah Kerr and William Windom) but is attracted to the woman. Trapped in a dead marriage, Elizabeth responds to Rettig, but although they make love she will not leave her husband to go with the flier on his endless, aimless travels around the country.

During the aerial show, where he is to perform a free-fall dive in which his parachute is released at the very last moment, the pointlessness of Rettig's life forces him to reappraise it. Prepared by his realization of its emptiness he allows himself to succumb to the morbid desire to die which periodically afflicts men who perform dangerous activities. Failing to pull the rip-cord, he plunges to his death in front of colleagues, crowd and the woman who is just the latest in a long line of casual lovers.

The show goes on and young Webson performs the same jump, then promptly quits, leaving Browdy, who has been wrestling with the decision of whether or not to accept an offer to work as a stuntman in Hollywood, free to make a success of his life.

The Brandons are left as they began, a man and woman caught in a sterile relationship with nothing to look forward to but lonely old age and death.

The pervading gloom reaches out and envelops the audience and it is difficult to care much for the Brandons and their fate, or even for Rettig as he approaches the end of his unhappy life.

These are basic faults of screenplay and direction. Without some knowledge and understanding of their personalities and backgrounds it is difficult to understand why, for example, Elizabeth refuses to leave her husband for Rettig. The fact that she senses that such a relationship would probably end badly is not in itself sufficient justification for not leaping at the chance to escape her stultifying life. Maybe it is simply natural inertia, which overcomes many people faced with such decisions, but if so it is not clear from the film.

Rettig's suicide, following Elizabeth's refusal to go away with him, makes sense only if this relationship can be seen as the last straw of many which ultimately break him, but the presence of these other straws is much too lightly intimated.

Although oppressively downbeat in its view of people's lives, *The Gypsy Moths* is saved from despondency by superbly-staged aerial sequences. Exciting and vivid, they show director John Frankenheimer to be completely at ease with machines even if, surprisingly given his television background, he is much less comfortable with the more intimate moments.

Best acting performance on view is Gene Hackman's as the member of the aerial trio with the most understandable if simplest personal crisis (should he desert his buddies and take the big chance being offered?).

The weekend's celebrations which form the backdrop to *The Gypsy Moths* were gloomily observed by Vincent Canby writing in the *New York Times*: 'It's a weekend of dimly articulated emotional crises for everyone, including Miss Kerr, an unhappy, highly unlikely Kansas housewife who has a brief affair with Lancaster, principally, you feel, because she remembers meeting him in *From Here to Eternity*.'

Despite the gloom of *The Gypsy Moths*, the bad reception given to *Castle Keep* and the failure of contemporary audiences to give *The Swimmer* its deserved due, Burt Lancaster could look back on the decade now ending with considerable satisfaction.

He had begun the 1960s with an Academy Award for *Elmer Gantry*, and he brought his introspective understanding to the role of Robert Stroud in *Birdman of Alcatraz*. Most important of all, he had given the finest performance of his career in *The Leopard*.

Measured in terms of his career, life could scarcely have been better. Unfortunatey, there was more to life than work and as the decade ended so his domestic life reached crisis point.

Although his marriage to Norma had survived many difficulties, time and her patience had run out.

The grounds on which she sued for divorce in July 1969 were mental cruelty, but most observers believed that it was Lancaster's compulsion to work which was largely instrumental in driving them apart. Then there were his relationships with other women. His wisecrack about always getting the girl, before or after his films were over, had enough truth to disturb the most tolerant of Hollywood wives.

Although neither Lancaster nor Norma made public statements about their divorce, she was granted custody of the three youngest children (the girls who were still minors) and received a substantial but undisclosed financial settlement.

Lancaster had a new companion, Jackie Bone, a former hairdresser who had made her first 'public' appearance on the set of *The Swimmer*.

In 1970 Lancaster renewed his long-held admiration for the work of the Civil Rights leader, the late Martin Luther King Jr, when he joined several other leading celebrities (including Charlton Heston, Paul Newman and Sidney Poitier) in narrating segments of a long documentary film directed jointly by Sidney Lumet and Joseph L. Mankiewicz, *King: A Filmed Record ... Montgomery to Memphis*.

For a while he contemplated selling his house in Bel-Air (which had been rebuilt after the fire). Instead he extended his property holdings when he allowed his developing love affair with Italy to take a practical turn with the acquisition of an apartment in Rome which he filled with elegant furnishings and a second art collection.

Despite his appreciation of the grandeur of Roman architecture and Italian operatic music of the past, in painting he inclined towards as yet unknown artists. He valued their work not for any potential monetary gain it might offer but for what he deemed to be its aesthetic worth.

The same cannot be said of his choice of film with which to herald the new decade. Artistic merit was noticeably absent in *Airport* (1970), a cliché-ridden disaster movie (although, in fairness, it might be remarked that not all the trite events in the film were then the clichés they later became as one appalling offspring followed another until 1980 when, hopefully, *Airplane* put an end to them).

Lancaster, as airport manager Mel Bakersfield, does what he is paid for but conveys the impression that he is less than wholly committed to the film. Indeed, he upset the makers by dismissing the entire $6 million affair (which became the top grossing film of all those in which he has appeared) as 'the biggest piece of junk ever made'.

On this particular shift at Lincoln International Airport, Bakersfield is beset by enough problems to paralyse any ordinary individual. An airliner has overrun the main runway and is now bogged down thus preventing any further movements on this strip. The secondary runway is too short for use in the prevailing bad weather and cannot, anyway, be used because local residents are protesting at noise levels.

Bakersfield is also having domestic problems: his wife wants a divorce, partly because he is married to his job but also because he isn't so married to it that he can't spare time for an affair with Tanya (Jean Seberg), the airport's passenger relations officer. His sister Sarah (Barbara Hale) is married to airline pilot Vern Demerest (Dean Martin) who is having an affair with stewardess Gwen Meighan (Jacqueline Bisset), now inconveniently pregnant.

Bakersfield decides to use the secondary runway despite objections while his head maintenance engineer (George Kennedy) attempts to move the stranded aircraft.

The first aircraft due to leave is the Rome flight piloted by Demerest and with Tanya among the cabin crew. Among the usual (for this kind of movie) cross-section of passengers on board is a demented failure, D.O. Guerrero (Van Heflin), whose luggage conceals a home-made bomb he plans to detonate in mid-air thus allowing his wife, Inez (Maureen Stapleton), to collect his life insurance.

If all this were not already more than enough for the airport to handle (to say nothing of the movie), Tanya's life is being made miserable by a little old lady, Ada Quonsett (Helen Hayes), who regularly stows away so that she can visit her far-flung daughter and indulge her love of flying – a delight that stops short of actually paying for a ticket.

The Rome flight takes off but Vern Demerest is alerted to the presence of the mad bomber whose wife has discovered his plan and called Mel Bakersfield. The pilot does his captain's best to talk sense into Guerrero but the bomb is inadvertently detonated, blowing a hole in the aircraft big enough to suck the bomber into space. Conveniently for everyone else, the hole doesn't prevent valiant Vern from bringing the airplane down safely. Once on the ground, Tanya is rushed to hospital where, presumably, she will have Demerest's baby who will grow up to take part in one of the film's sequels.

Based upon Arthur Hailey's immaculately researched novel, the film's background is suitably authentic but, much as in Hailey's novels, the characters tend to be swamped in a mass of swirling detail. Cardboard cut-out and stereotyped as these characters are, none of the performers is given a fair chance to act although Helen Hayes, as the irresponsible geriatric stowaway, does well enough as do George Kennedy, Barbara Hale and Maureen Stapleton.

As the would-be saboteur, Van Heflin twitches his way over the top, a surprising trait in so practised a performer. Perhaps he knew that *Airport* was to be his last film before his death in 1971 and didn't much care any more.

Jean Seberg, an actress greatly misused in films as she was in real life, barely gets by as does Dean Martin while Jacqueline Bissett is wooden, a characteristic she shrugged off only later in her career when she matured from being merely a decorative star into a skilled and effective actress.

From the ups and downs of life in a contemporary airport, Lancaster travelled backwards in time and westwards in direction to make another clutch of superior (if not too successful) westerns.

Although each of the three is different in content and concept, they possess certain similarities in that all strive, generally successfully, for depth and a level of integrity not found in the average horse opera.

In *Lawman* (1971) US Marshal Jered Maddox (Lancaster) arrives in the town of Sabbath to arrest seven men who shot up his own town, accidentally killing an old man in the process. Given the circumstances, if the seven men return freely with Maddox they are likely to face only a fine or a couple of nights in jail. But the seven have grown accustomed to a different breed of lawman to the implacable Maddox.

Marshal of Sabbath is Cotton Ryan (Robert Ryan), a former gunfighter who has lost his ability and spirit, his honour and self-respect, and is in the pay of Vincent Bronson (Lee J. Cobb). The man who 'owns' Sabbath and who also employs most of the seven men, Bronson is a throwback to past times when big ranchers were little gods. Unfortunately for the rancher and his men, Marshal Maddox is also a throwback.

Proud and stubborn, a man of principle even if his principles cause him to begin the merciless extinction of the seven men for refusing to give themselves up, Maddox unfalteringly metes out his own brand of unnecessarily extreme justice.

An old girlfriend, Laura Shelby (Sheree North), pleads with Maddox to leave town as her man, Hurd Price (J.D. Cannon), is one of the doomed seven. If he dies she will have even less than she has now and all that she has now is a share in a dessicated and worthless patch of land she and Price try to cultivate. But Maddox is deaf to her pleas; whatever he and Laura might have had in the past, no spark remains.

Bronson attempts to change Maddox's mind. The old rancher has spent a lifetime building his empire and doesn't want to see it wasted, but Maddox ignores him too. The law is the law and he is its upholder. No one, not even Bronson who owns one tame lawman, is above the law.

One by one, Maddox confronts the men he wants and when they resist he kills them. He has ceased to be merely a US marshal; now he is judge, jury and executioner. He has become the Law.

As the remaining members of the group gather to defend themselves against the inexorable Maddox, Bronson's son is killed. Distraught, Bronson puts his own gun into his mouth and kills himself. Hurd Price throws down his gun and runs away, screaming for mercy. Although he knows that Laura Shelby is watching him, Maddox shoots Price in the back.

Skilfully constructed, with an excellent script by Gerald Wilson, the film is tautly directed by Michael Winner. The morality of the story occasionally suggests an underlying brutality of mind and purpose with an overlay of cold cynicism (a trait for which Winner is frequently condemned), but reflection suggests that there is more morality here than meets the eye.

Winner's world is frequently bleak and like many others he has been tempted into financially secure sequels following a successful original. Whatever the demerits of his *Death Wish* series overall, the first film in the series reacted with a powerful primitive emotion which many thought had been sloughed off by advancing civilization. What the gut response to the film proved, and what Winner had clearly understood all along, was that society's need for simplistic vengeance was barely buried beneath the glossy surface and was ready to burst into violent life with only the slightest provocation.

The cold-blooded morality displayed by Jered Maddox was far from outmoded by changes in society in the last hundred years. The brutal killing of Hurd Price does have its point. Maddox is a man of principle and although one of his tenets is never to shoot a man in the back, he can kill Price in this way because the fleeing man represents weakness and cowardice – two characteristics totally foreign to this dedicated lawman. Killing Price is a form of retribution against the kind of man who has replaced Maddox's world with another softer and seemingly more civilized world in which nothing is secure or predictable and in which morality is an old-fashioned and meaningless word. It is also a more deadly world although in it death comes from vastly more dangerous places than the barrel of a Colt .45.

Performances in *Lawman* are solid throughout. Lee J. Cobb (at Winner's insistence without a toupee for the first time in his career) brings anguished dichotomy to the rancher who wants peace but cannot bend the iron will he needed to build an empire here in the wilderness. The minor roles are all soundly played. Sheree North is vulnerable and pathetic and always believable. Among other fine performances are Joseph Wiseman as an enigmatic cripple from Maddox's past who saves the Marshal's life, John McGiver as the ear-trumpet-toting town mayor, and J.D. Cannon as the inherently peaceful Hurd Price who has been sucked into a maelstrom of violence beyond his capacity for understanding. As Cotton Ryan, the disillusioned Marshal of Sabbath who has sold out in order to live in peace, Robert Ryan is particularly effective in finding the right touch of shamed acknowledgement of his weaknesses.

Lancaster's Jered Maddox is a powerful man, quiet and purposeful, with an undercurrent of violence always bubbling beneath the surface. He allows only the barest hint to show that he is aware that within himself lie the very qualities that he despises in others, qualities which at most times he is at pains to bury but which must in the end surface in violence and death.

It is another fine introspective performance and enhances a film of considerable dramatic impact.

The introspection and fidelity of purpose displayed by Jered Maddox were characteristics common to Lancaster's next western role.

In *Valdez is Coming* (1971) he is again a lawman; this time Bob Valdez, a tired and dusty ageing Mexican deputy in a border town where the local people are in thrall to a powerful rancher, Frank Tanner (Jon Cypher).

Valdez confronts Tanner and his men in a doomed attempt to collect a few dollars for the pregnant widow of a man they have killed (mistakenly believing him to be a murderer).

Valdez is humiliated by Tanner, beaten, crucified and thrown off the ranch.

Despite such treatment, Valdez does not seek revenge for his humiliation and beating; all he wants is a few dollars for the pregnant Indian woman. Decking himself out in the uniform he wore long ago as a US Cavalry scout, he gives a friend a message to be passed on to the white men at the hacienda: 'Tell them Valdez is coming.'

After kidnapping Tanner's mistress Gay Erin (Susan Clark), Valdez takes to the mountains into which he is trailed by Tanner and his men who grow increasingly reluctant as Valdez begins picking them off with a buffalo gun with awesome range.

Alone in the wilderness with this softly spoken man of integrity, the rancher's mistress is soon attracted to him and they become lovers.

Eventually, Valdez is surrounded and Frank Tanner orders his execution but his men have begun to see the quiet Mexican differently. Slowly, all the rancher's men turn away until Tanner alone stands there. The lawman repeats the simple request which precipitated all the preceding bloodletting; all he wants is a few dollars for the pregnant widow.

The story-line, with its undertones of racism and corruption (among other things it is intimated that Tanner murdered his best friend and partner in order to take his land and his wife), is carried along well by the action sequences. The film is never bogged down in wordiness, offering its moral messages with commendable simplicity.

In the slow build-up in violence, when only a minor concession by one side is needed, the film is reminiscent of *Lawman*. In other respects too both films have something to say about the human condition which far outstrips their Hollywood western format.

All the performances are sound but this is essentially a one-character film. In lesser hands this might have resulted in sagging during the quieter moments but Lancaster holds it together, providing a strong if silent central core. It is another of his understated, reflective performances and his personal commitment to liberal ideals gleams through the grimy exterior of the proud but down-at-heel Mexican lawman.

The inclusion of a strand of racism in the fabric of films was not uncommon in the 1970s and just as this element was woven into *Valdez is Coming*, so a similar but stronger thread formed the *raison d'être* and the main strength of Lancaster's next film.

Ulzana's Raid (1972) brought Lancaster and director Robert Aldrich together for the first time since 1954 when they had made *Apache* and *Vera Cruz*. This time, however, with the Vietnam war in every American mind, their aim was to achieve much more than either of the earlier collaborations.

Ulzana's Raid recounts the exploits of a US Cavalry platoon commanded by young Lieutenant Garnett De Buin (Bruce Davison) and guided by McIntosh (Lancaster) an old, cynical but wise scout.

The platoon is sent out in pursuit of a band of Apaches led by the much-feared Ulzana (Joaquin Martinez) who have broken out of the reservation to which they have been confined by the US government.

What begins as a routine calvary-and-Indian chase soon develops manifold undertones (which were hopelessly complicated for audiences by drastic editing which sabotaged the director's intentions). Using the US government's treatment of the Native Americans in the nineteenth century as its text, the film attempts to look at the actions of twentieth-century politicians engaged in a hopeless conflict in south-east Asia.

It is the display of error and uncertainty among the soldiers, their lack of understanding of just what they are supposed to be doing in these alien surroundings, and their blind hatred of the unknown, that turns Ulzana's group of renegades into a representation of the Viet Cong. Director Aldrich does not deny the sometimes murderous intent of these men; instead he makes it clear that this is their land and they will defend it by whatever means are necessary.

Ulzana's Apaches are launched on a terrifying campaign of plunder, torture, rape and murder. Some of the killings are extremely brutal and one in particular is lingered upon in grisly detail. Rukeyser (Karl Swenson), an immigrant settler, is alone in his cabin surrounded by Ulzana's band, having sent his wife and son to safety. (In fact, Rukeyser's family and their army

'McIntosh', the cynical but wise old scout in *Ulzana's Raid* (1972)

'Cross' and Paul Scofield find the quiet corners in the world of
espionage depicted in *Scorpio* (1973)

Discussing the finer points of directing with Michael Winner

'Farrington' and Robert Ryan prepare to commit the
unthinkable crime in *Executive Action* (1973). (Below) Robert
Ryan nearing the end of his career and his life celebrates
completing work on *The Outfit* (1973) with Jane Russell,
Lancaster and Joanna Cassidy

'The Professor' finds small compensations when his life is disrupted by Claudia Marsani in *Conversation Piece* (1975)

'General Lawrence Dell' prepares to launch atomic missiles in *Twilight's Last Gleaming* (1977) while Paul Winfield tries hard to deflect his aims

Yet another experiment by 'Dr Moreau' in his obsessive search for genetic perfection in *The Island of Dr Moreau* (1977)

Hard-bitten 'Major Asa Barker', a professional to the end in *Go Tell the Spartans* (1978)

A moment of tranquility for 'Colonel Durnford', Simon Ward
and Anna Calder-Marshall before the bloody battles of
Zulu Dawn (1979)

'Lou Pascal' and Susan Sarandon see his moment of triumph
on the nine o'clock news in *Atlantic City* (1980)

'Felix Happer' comes briefly down to earth with Fulton Mackay
in *Local Hero* (1983)

'Carl Julius Deutz' hands on the dynasty to a new and terrible generation in *Sins of The Fathers* (1986), with Dieter Laser

Revitalized by their adventures in *Atlantic City* (1980), 'Lou Pascal' and Kate Reid face a happier future

escort have already fallen victim to the Apache, the escort killing the woman to save her from a worse fate before shooting himself.) Ulzana and his men have gathered on a ridge overlooking Rukeyser's cabin and one of them raises a bugle, a trophy of some earlier battle. Relief glows in the settler's eyes as he hears the sound but the audience, enlightened also by intercut shots of the still far-distant cavalry, knows better.

When De Buin and his troops and the veteran scout reach the cabin, the manner of Rukeyser's death is revealed. Bound and helpless, a fire lit upon his stomach, Rukeyser clearly took a long time to die.

Horrified, the young officer questions how a group of supposed human beings could kill a man in this way. Wearily, McIntosh explains: the Apache believe that a man's strength and courage pass to his killer. The longer a man takes to die, the greater his strength and courage and thus the more he has to pass on to those who take his life. The primitive logic of this is beyond the young officer's comprehension and the incident serves only to fan the fire of his already consuming hatred for the men he sees as savages.

What the old scout sees, and what the audience is encouraged to understand by director Aldrich, is that here is a society which differs so utterly from the white man's own that it cannot be judged by alien standards. Only by looking at the Apache through Apache eyes can such behaviour be understood. Maybe it will never be condoned or even grudgingly accepted, but it is at least a tentative step along a difficult road which leads towards a measure of understanding. It will take time, generations certainly, and there will always be those who will never bridge the gap, but if the attempt is not made then the future will hold still more bloody conflicts.

Among the film's many messages is that men cannot begin to coexist with people of other cultures without abolishing hatred from their minds and replacing it with understanding, and, if that is not possible, at least with tolerance for their differences. Respect for an enemy was a staple ingredient of many World War II gung-ho adventures where it was often indicated by the merest suspicion of a tear in a battle-hardened eye when the killing was over. In a much more sophisticated approach, Aldrich is saying that by respecting cultural differences it might be possible to stop men from becoming enemies in the first place.

This is not to suggest that easy answers are offered by the director. Loose ends abound with the ending a deliberate hodgepodge of errors caused through inexperience and incompetence among the participants in the final confrontation between cavalry and Apache.

There are in existence different versions of *Ulzana's Raid* and anyone reading the foregoing should be aware that the version released theatrically in America and shown on British television differs in numerous, subtle but highly significant ways from the so-called 'foreign version' released into non-American cinemas. A closely detailed analysis of the differences can be found in the July and August issues of *Monthly Film Bulletin*. This analysis demonstrates how extra footage and additional but differing takes of individual scenes can be used to vary a film-maker's intentions.

John Ford was noted for the way in which he shot only that which was needed for his vision of the films he made. He seldom concerned himself with what editors, producers or studio heads did to his footage, secure in the knowledge that he had given them little room for manoeuvre. Ford's lesson was a valuable one and remains so today. It is one to which more directors should pay heed if they have a serious and committed viewpoint they wish to impart to their audience. This is especially important when a director like Aldrich seeks to convey some of the anger he clearly feels on a subject which seared the collective conscience of America in the 1970s. Not that Aldrich's anger was an immature outpouring; far from it in fact. For as Harry Ringel pointed out in an article on the director in the September 1974 issue of *Take One*, men do not 'make films *about* anger, as opposed to angry ones, without first learning not to hate'.

Lancaster's performance in *Ulzana's Raid* is skilled and thoughtful. As the softly spoken, ever-watchful ageing scout he is never critical of the inexperience of others. He casts a powerful shadow over the film, even in the few moments when he is not on screen.

The end, as he lies against a boulder, fatally wounded but calmly accepting his fate, echoes an attitude which appears in other films he has made. He has no death wish, but seeing the way his world has developed into one with standards and attitudes he cannot accommodate, he doesn't particularly want to go on living in it.

Certainly, he has no wish to exist in a world in which he has no choice over which men he shall call his enemy. And if he did, it seems unlikely that he would choose the Apache for this role even if that is what they really are.

The name Apache is not a designation of an Indian nation as is, say, Kiowa or Cheyenne. 'Apache' is the word used by other Indian nations to describe a nameless band of warlike nomads who roamed the south-western reaches of the continent. The word means 'enemy' but, as the film makes clear, although the Viet Cong might have been Apache to the American army during the Vietnam war so the American soldier was Apache to the Viet Cong.

Something of the depths of *Ulzana's Raid* was observed by Vincent Canby writing in the *New York Times*. 'Aldrich's West is a timeless place where noble motives lead to disastrous actions. Loyalties are hopelessly confused and the only possible satisfaction in life is behaving well for the immediate moment. This Burt Lancaster does with ease, along with … the rest of the predominantly male cast.'

The wisdom of Lancaster's scout might well have been heeded by those who prolonged the war in Vietnam. Several times, he talks to the young lieutenant about the futility of hatred: 'Hating the Apaches would be like hating the desert because there ain't no water in it … You might as well hate the wind … Stop hating and start thinking.'

And when the soldiers seek to kill with mindless violence, he makes an observation that shines light upon the refusal of many Americans to believe the truths of My Lai and other actions: 'What bothers you, Lieutenant, is that you don't like to think of white men behaving like Indians; it kind of confuses the issue.'

Political attitudes expressed in outwardly non-political films do not necessarily reflect a participating actor's point of view. However, during the early 1970s Lancaster's own stance was clearly anti-war. He acted as an usher at a 1972 fund-raising function held in Los Angeles for Senator George McGovern, an early and outspoken opponent of the Vietnam war.

Around the same time, Lancaster's interest in public affairs was displayed by his participation as narrator for a number of controversial television commercials. Made on behalf of consumer groups, one of these concerned the potentially dangerous flaws in Chevrolet motor cars, another revealed hazards inherent in certain pain-relieving drugs.

In 1971 Lancaster made a brief but explosive return to the stage when he played the lead in a musical for a summer season in San Francisco and Los Angeles.

Originally written in 1938 by Maxwell Anderson and Kurt Weill for actor Walter Huston, *Knickerbocker Holiday* demands a dominating central performance. As Peter Stuyvesant, the military governor of New Amsterdam (later New York), Lancaster sang and danced with an attractive mixture of charm and aggression. Equipped with a silver peg-leg (his own left leg strapped up painfully behind him), he gyrated enthusiastically and delighted the audience by swinging across the stage on a trapeze.

Perhaps the pleasure the show brought to audiences lucky enough to see it was matched by Lancaster's own delight in at last being allowed to sing professionally. A Kurt Weill score, with such songs as 'The Scars' and the evocative 'September Song', was as close as he was ever able to come to his beloved opera. That he took his singing seriously can be seen from the fact that he sought advice from Frank Sinatra who coached him prior to the opening of the show.

When Lancaster returned to the screen it was into a very different world from that of the recent westerns and the stage musical, even though all of these did have political undertones. *Scorpio* (1973), which brought him into the uncertain world of international espionage, was deeply political.

Cross (Lancaster) is a middle-aged CIA agent who has somehow survived changes of government, control and attitudes. The mere fact of Cross's survival prompts his cynical boss, McLeod (John Colicos), to conclude that he must be a double-agent and he orders his death as a purely precautionary measure.

The assigned hit-man is Laurier, code-named 'Scorpio' (Alain Delon), who learned his trade from his intended victim.

At first Scorpio declines the job but is framed on a phoney

drugs bust by the unscrupulous McLeod. Faced with a thirty-year prison sentence, Scorpio reluctantly agrees to kill his former teacher and friend.

Realizing that he is under surveillance and guessing the probable outcome, Cross decides to run. In Vienna he meets up with an old adversary, KGB agent Zharkov (Paul Scofield), with whom he enjoys bonds of old comradeship forged in the Spanish Civil War.

Hotly pursued by Scorpio and CIA agents of varying degrees of incompetence, Cross prepares for the final run to safety. By now he is being shadowed by the Russians who have decided that they too want him – but alive not dead. Cross enlists Zharkov's aid, his old adversary delightedly framing his own party-line superior into backing off from the harassed American.

Meanwhile, in Washington, McLeod orders a search of Cross's home in the hope of finding proof that his intended victim really is a traitor. The searchers are disturbed by Cross's wife, Sarah (Joanne Linville), and she is killed by a CIA agent.

When Zharkov learns of this he tells Cross who immediately returns to Washington where he contacts Pick (Melvin Stewart), the friend who helped him leave the country. This time, Pick helps set up an ambush in which Cross kills McLeod.

McLeod's successor as head of the CIA, Filchock (J.D. Cannon), urges Scorpio to complete his mission but the younger man is now even more certain that Cross is not a double-agent. Persuaded to study the 'evidence' again, Scorpio runs a film made of Sarah's activities while Cross was in Vienna. As the film unrolls, Scorpio sees his own girlfriend, Susan (Gayle Hunnicutt), and realizes that all along she has been working with Cross.

At last fully co-operative in the plan to kill Cross, now that he has a personal reason, Scorpio goes in pursuit of the older man. He finds him with Susan in an underground car-park and kills them both, but then, as he comes up into the street, Scorpio is shot down by a CIA agent hidden in the shadows.

Although receiving the generally unfavourable reviews critics reserve for films directed by Michael Winner, *Scorpio* is much more than just another espionage tale. Even at that basic level it is very good with the chase sequences well worked out and executed. Usually, however, routine cloak-and-dagger dramas have cardboard cut-out characters. That does not apply here. With one or two minor exceptions (Scorpio's girlfriend is one), the characters are well-rounded and entirely believable if the premise of duplicity and incompetence within the world's leading intelligence organizations is accepted. Coming as it did, hard on top of Watergate, the validity of this facet of *Scorpio* can hardly be denied.

Robin Bean, writing in *Sight & Sound* (November 1973), commented that 'technically, for anyone interested in the art of film-making, it is a must since the technique is pretty near flawless – the construction and the editing are a delight, as is the harsh realistic lighting of Robert Paynter.' (Cinematographer Paynter had worked on Winner's previous film with Lancaster, *Lawman*, as did Gerald Wilson who co-wrote the screenplay for *Scorpio* with David Rintels.)

As often happens in Winner's films, there are few real heroes. Only three people in *Scorpio* deserve sympathy and affection: Cross, Zharkov and Cross's wife. Everyone else is either untrustworthy, duplicitous, shallow or just plain murderous. A few of the minor characters are likeable but these (Pick, for example) are either criminals or society's outcasts.

There are many good performances in *Scorpio*. Among the most commendable is Joanne Linville's interpretation of the role of Cross's wife. Relatively dialogue-free, the role is of considerable importance since much of the film's denouement depends upon how Cross reacts to her death. A lesser performance in this easily overlooked role would have severely weakened the film.

John Colicos and J.D. Cannon, as the CIA chiefs, exude shifty-eyed greasy authority with enough conviction to make wary those living in a world in which a real-life former CIA chief now has his finger on half of the world's atomic buttons.

Melvin Stewart is excellent as Cross's criminal friend who has a better sense of right and wrong than any of the government agents with whom he is surrounded. Like most black actors, Stewart was usually refused important roles but comfortably carried the load of a shared lead in *Trick Baby* (1973).

As Scorpio, Alain Delon has the right amount of coolly clinical detachment for the role of an assassin although some of his lines suffer from being delivered in what is for him a foreign language. He speaks English well but sometimes his inflections and phrasing unbalance the lines he has to deliver.

As the two ageing spies, Scofield and Lancaster are a delight. Unlike their previous film, *The Train*, here they are given several scenes together without which little of what surrounds them would have the same quality of reality. Zharkov and Cross are not mere ciphers in the hands of faceless governments; they are real men with pasts and presents and dreams of futures. The changing world surrounding them is displayed in a scene where Zharkov says, 'Have you noticed, Cross, that we are being replaced by younger men with bright, stupid faces, a sense of fashion and a dedication to nothing more than efficiency. Keepers of machines. Pushers of buttons. Hardware men with highly complex toys and except for language not an iota of difference between the American model and the Soviet model.'

Cross, smiling serenely, nods his agreement to this and raises his glass in a toast: 'To dinosaurs.'

Later as the two men get merrily drunk, Cross comments upon the nature of their work and how they have truly outlived their original purpose. 'There are no more secrets', he says. 'At least none worth stealing.'

When time finally runs out for Cross and Scorpio catches up with him, he makes no attempt to escape. With his wife already dead, accidentally murdered by his own people, and knowing himself to be an anachronistic embarrassment to the government for which he has spent a lifetime stealing and lying and cheating, he truly has nothing left to live for.

Between the first shot from Scorpio's gun, which badly wounds him, and the second which ends his life, Cross can summarize the whole messy business that has been his life for more than thirty years.

'There's a room just down the hall from McLeod's office; a room where they're going to play a game. It's a bit like Monopoly; only more people get hurt. There's no good and no bad ... the object is not to win but not to lose; and the only rule is to stay in the game.'

In his scenes with Joanne Linville, as Sarah his wife, in his death scene with Delon, but most especially in the marvellous moments with Paul Scofield, Lancaster uses his art to perfection.

He is always believable, commands attention and sympathy, and admirably holds his own with Scofield which alone is no mean feat.

Whether or not the real world of international espionage is like director Michael Winner's world in *Scorpio* is not important. What matters here is that it appears to be right. As more and yet more evidence of governmental intrigue and corruption emerges in America, Britain and almost everywhere else it is sad to reflect that Winner's world is probably closer to reality than even he knew at the time he made this film.

For his next film Lancaster remained in the demi-world of political corruption, working on a film for which he, and all other participants, drew only minimum scale.

Set in 1963, *Executive Action* (1973) is an imaginative account of what might have lain behind the assassination of President John F. Kennedy.

A group of powerful right-wing American businessmen gather to plot the death of the man they believe will prove instrumental in destroying their financial interests if allowed to pursue his policies unchecked.

In this version of the conspiracy theory, these dangerous reactionaries hire Farrington (Lancaster), a disaffected CIA agent, who in turn hires teams of marksmen as arrangements are made to redirect the presidential motorcade during a forthcoming visit Kennedy will make to Dallas.

The story-line of the film then broadly follows known facts but mixes reasonable conclusion with wild supposition – and occasionally outright fiction – to form a blend which sometimes works very well. Where it falls down is in such loose ends as the almost random selection and dimly-articulated motivation of Farrington and his teams of gunmen. Nor is the motivation of the right-wing businessmen led by Foster (Robert Ryan) sufficiently well defined unless the audience supplies the unstated assumption that these men were somehow assured that on Kennedy's death his successor in the White House would at once abandon significant planks in his political platform. Such a commitment would, of course, hint at connivance, at the highest level, in the plot and, given the date of its making, such a statement by the film's makers might well have been ill-advised.

In some scenes, the manner in which fact and fiction, deduction and speculation are tied together is frequently awkward. For example, the visit to Jack Ruby by an anonymous agent, presumably to set up Ruby's subsequent killing of Lee Harvey Oswald, Kennedy's alleged sole assassin, is not explicated. The audience is left to draw its own conclusion but has been given no choice what that conclusion should be. In fact, of all aspects of the assassination and the plethora of conspiracy theories that came in its wake, Jack Ruby's remains one of the most obstinately inexplicable. He doesn't fit the presumed profile of a loyal citizen temporarily deranged through grief but neither does it seem likely that a group of thoroughly organized conspirators, wanting Oswald silenced, would have chosen someone as unstable and potentially unreliable as Ruby. Ruby's death from natural causes soon after the events described in *Executive Action* clouded the issue still further while, in 1989, long after the making of the film, revelations of Ruby's relationship with members of the local police made it even harder to obtain a clear view of his role.

Other events of the late 1980s, among them the uncovering of the 'Marseilles Connection', further muddied the waters – this time probably beyond redemption.

Dalton Trumbo's screenplay follows a story by Donald Freed and Mark Lane (whose book, *Rush to Judgement*, rightly cast doubt upon the Warren Commission's report on the assassination and concluded that Oswald was the sole perpetrator). Both screenplay and David Miller's direction fudge many of the awkward areas, perhaps out of concern for what might have happened if their film was too outspoken.

As a result, the film, like Lane's book, removes most credibility from the official version of Kennedy's assassination while failing to put anything stronger in its place.

At the end of the film the group of rich businessmen gathers in gloomy celebration of its success. News comes that Farrington has died of a heart attack. Whether his end was truly from natural causes is made doubtful by a closing title sequence which lists all the real people, central and peripheral to the events in Dallas in November 1963, who died in the months following Kennedy's death. Some of the deaths were suspicious, some merely made to seem so by implication. The film does not justify these implications.

None of the main characters in *Executive Action* is sufficiently well drawn to give the actors much to get their teeth into. As a consequence, the (so far as is known wholly imaginary) scenes of the macabre rehearsals for the assassination with pictures of Kennedy as targets carry more weight than should really be the case. The caper has taken over from the message and the entire film suffers.

Peter Cargin, writing in *Film 74*, commented that Lancaster and Ryan do in fact blend quite successfully into the anonymous 'documentary air that director David Miller has conceived for his film'. Penelope Houston, in *Monthly Film Bulletin* (January 1974) remarked on the twin strands of fact and fiction and described the fictitious strand as 'a spare, thinly characterized account of meetings and deliberations among a group who are seen less as ruthless machinators than as mournful, almost doomed figures driven by destiny towards the slaughter of their own Caesar.'

The character of Foster, the arch-conspirator, is wearily manifested by the terminally-ill Robert Ryan. He appears as a man resigned to carrying out the unthinkable homicide in order to avoid having to adjust to an unpalatable future. (This was Ryan's penultimate film role and he was dead before *Executive Action* was released.)

Despite his billing, Lancaster's role in the film is restricted as events, rather than people, take precedence. He does what he can with the role of a man who might or might not have existed in real life but the absence of credible motivation cuts the ground from under him.

Back in the mid 1950s Lancaster had tried his hand at directing a film but had avoided repeating this activity ever since he had discovered that it wasn't quite as easy as it looked from the other side of the camera. The passage of two decades must have caused the problems he'd encountered on that occasion to fade a little from his mind because now – a little unwisely as it turned out – he decided to tackle the job again.

7   Law and Politics

When, after directing *The Kentuckian*, Burt Lancaster declared that if he directed again he wouldn't star, it was good advice. He should have listened more closely to himself because *The Midnight Man* (1974) – in which he was not only star and director, but also writer and producer – never really lifts off.

Lancaster gamely tackled these multiple roles but perceptibly bit off more than he could reasonably have expected to chew even if he did have collaborative help from Roland Kibbee.

The book upon which *The Midnight Man* is based is a densely plotted tale of corruption and betrayal. In adapting the novel for the screen, co-writers Lancaster and Kibbee rightly sought to effect some simplification, but in the event they appear to have been insufficiently ruthless and unnecessary complications remain.

Set on a university campus, the story centres on former cop Jim Slade (Lancaster) who has recently ended a prison term for murdering his wife's lover. Slade is now trying to hold down a job as a security guard. As the title suggests, he works the graveyard shift and an air of middle-of-the-night depression hangs over everything.

Despite the simplification of David Anthony's novel, the cumbersome plot requires much of the film's energies to be absorbed in wading through piles of exposition. Slade's voice-over at the end is an indication of how much plot was left to unravel when time and patience – or the money – ran out.

Considering the strong cast on hand, it is unfortunate that the potential for an atmospheric dissection of both small-town corruption and college campus intrigue is largely dissipated.

Lancaster does well enough but his role is an uneasy one, carrying as it does the burdensome problem of trying to be incorruptibly pure and honest while swimming through a cesspool of sexual and moral depravity. Some of the muck should have stuck. It was a problem which did not exist in the novel because the Jim Slade character there is a private eye with no illusions about his own or anyone else's morality.

As if to recover from the tribulations of directing himself, for his next film Lancaster returned to working with a director for whom he had great respect and admiration following their joint artistic triumph with *The Leopard*.

Since that earlier collaboration Luchino Visconti had been gravely ill and *Conversation Piece* (1975) was his first film after returning to work.

Essentially a single-set film, the story presents a microcosm of contemporary Italian life wherein a lonely intellectual finds his peaceful life upended when new neighbours move into an adjoining apartment.

The single set is a house in Rome owned by an American professor (Lancaster) who studies the history of art, especially English portraits of family groups known as conversation pieces. (The original Italian title of the film was *Gruppo di Famiglia in un Interno*.)

Into the professor's lonely retreat come Countess Bianca Brumonti (Silvana Mangano), her daughter Lietta (Claudia Marsani), and the countess's lover, Konrad Hübel (Helmut Berger). The newcomers have no evil intent, they are simply self-centred individuals who believe that the world owes them a place and a living and see no reason why the professor should not provide both.

Inevitably, Lancaster's central role in *Conversation Piece* has been contrasted with his role in his other film for Visconti. Here, as in *The Leopard*, he is a man coming towards the end of his life and attempting to come to terms not only with this but also the realization that the world he has known is ending. Once again, Visconti's suggestion is that of the two, perhaps death is marginally preferable to living on amidst the disappearance of those values which have signposted the character's life. It is a gloomy view and while it might have prevailed in the fading grandeur of the earlier film, here there is much less conviction.

Although Lancaster had previously refused roles with strong religious connotations (Elmer Gantry apart), his next film which was also made in Italy plunged him into a major production as mankind's greatest (and possibly most-ignored) law-giver. In tackling the role of Moses, Lancaster contradicted the attitude which had prompted him to refuse the title role in *Ben Hur*. This time, his decision to make an overtly religious film was fired by the combination of a screenplay he admired and the opportunity to portray a man who argued with God.

A television co-production, *Moses* (1976) features a multi-national cast with all the attendant problems such ventures bring in their wake. (Originally screened by CBS between 21 June and 2 August 1975, the series was edited into feature film length and released theatrically the following year.)

Not least of the film's problems lies in the fact that international film-makers seem unaware that actors work best when they can hear, think about and respond to what is being said to them by their fellow actors.

It is a pity that *Moses* is plagued with this particular hardship, besides which frogs and locusts are no trouble at all, because as these and other film-makers have shown, there are greater possibilities to the Old Testament than even Cecil B. DeMille ever reached at his most overwrought.

Lancaster's portrayal of Moses has all the strength and determination needed for the part of the man who led the chosen people out of bondage in Egypt and he helps hold together a tale which is always in danger of disintegrating into a collection of dramatic anecdotes.

The supporting players, including Anthony Quayle as Aaron, Ingrid Thulin as Miriam and Irene Papas as Zipporah, cope well but the soundtrack language-mix does none of them any kindness. (Lancaster's son, William, plays Moses as a young man.)

For the third film in a row, Lancaster worked in Italy, this time with Bernardo Bertolucci on a major production which sought to capitalize upon the director's unexpected commercial success with *Last Tango in Paris* (1972).

Novacento (1976) is a wide-ranging, visionary exploration of Italy's recent history told through the lives of two boys born on the same day and in the same place in Italy. The day is at the turn of the century, the place the northern region of Emilia which was the cradle of Italian socialism.

One of the boys is heir to the vast landholdings built up by Alfredo Belinghieri (Lancaster); the other is the grandson of Leo Dalco (Sterling Hayden), leader of the local peasant community which work the lands.

Unlike Visconti's vision of Italy in *The Leopard*, where the survival of the Prince was a matter of an individual's determination to adjust to a changing society, in Bertolucci's view it is society which adjusts and compromises to accommodate the individual whose survival is almost a matter of chance.

Although just as opposed to one another as their grandsons become, the two old men have differing views of the scheme of things. Despite coming from opposite ends of the social and economic scale, they are much closer in spirit and ideology than either would admit, even if either was aware of their resemblance.

Pauline Kael, writing in the *New Yorker*, likened them to giants drawn from the era of the American western film but in many respects they owe their origins to less romantic but equally deep-rooted stereotypes.

The craftsman employee (represented by Leo) is filled with a desire to do his work well and overcomes any tendency to recognize the harshly imposed reality of his station in life. The feudal employer (Alfredo) is benignly paternalistic and firmly believes that he knows what is best for 'his' people.

These stereotypical attitudes towards life are reflected in the manner in which the two old men die. Leo Dalco sits down by a tree to gaze out across the land to which he has devoted a lifetime of unremitting toil and quietly falls into his last sleep. Alfredo chooses the manner of his death; even if a filthy stable is an unpleasant place in which a man should hang himself, he achieves a kind of morbid dignity through his act. (Cuts made in this film by the Italian censor confuse the motive for suicide. Originally, it related more to Alfredo's despair at a failed attempt at sexual intimacy with a young woman than to an abstract philosophy of life and death.)

The film opens on 25 April 1945, Liberation Day, then flashes back to earlier times. Two young boys, Alfredo and Olmo, grandsons of old Alfredo and Leo grow to adulthood (Robert De

Niro and Gérard Depardieu) with Alfredo inheriting the family estates and becoming a passive fascist and Olmo embracing nascent Italian socialism.

On an earthier level both young men become involved with women; Alfredo marries Ada (Dominique Sanda), a French girl, while Olmo lives with Anita (Stefania Sandrelli), a fellow socialist, until her death in childbirth.

Alfredo and Olmo live through all the important events in modern Italian history: the peasant revolt of 1908, World War I, the rise of fascism and the Fascist government of 1922, World War II, and the nation's subsequent liberation from the fascist tyranny which had blighted a generation.

Alfredo's passive acceptance of fascism is only one example of his complaisant attitude towards the world. He tolerates the manner in which his foreman, Attila (Donald Sutherland), tyrannizes over the workers on his land because he believes that things are as they are and always will be. His view, that neither he nor anyone else can change the status quo is ultimately vindicated when, on Liberation Day, he is found guilty by a people's court which is powerless to punish him. Alfredo and his kind will go on exactly as before.

For the most part the broad sweep of Bertolucci's vision is always sustained and owes much to the work of cinematographer Vittorio Storaro who gives the soft golden countryside a warm, diffuse welcoming look. In this respect the film can be likened to Visconti's *The Leopard* although in their respective philosophies the two are very different.

A measure of insecurity in the film's direction allied to the occasional inability of the actors to dominate the landscape within which their characters live out their lives creates unfortunate unevenness.

That the actors have problems is strange given that the principal carriers of the action are De Niro and Depardieu, both strong and gifted players. Their failure to take hold and command suggests that at some point during production Bertolucci suffered a sudden loss of confidence in his ability to complete what he had begun. Instead of etching the De Niro and Depardieu characters sharply, so that they are delineated clearly amidst the broader brush strokes depicting the major events that form the backdrop to their lives, he allows them to fade into the scenery. It is an odd failing because he doesn't make the same mistake with either Hayden or Lancaster, nor even with the minor characters. Indeed, as Attila the fascist, Donald Sutherland is allowed to get away with a moustache-twirling send up of all the big bad villains in film history.

The coarsely drawn and balefully stereotyped Attila is matched in his oversimplifications by Alfredo and Olmo. The former is weak and sexually subdued; the latter is pure and honest, potent and commanding. Such stereotyping works directly against De Niro and Depardieu because these particular actors, by their customary internalizing of their roles, vanish beneath the surface. One unfortunate result of this is that, try as one might to forget it, Sutherland's outrageous camping sticks awkwardly in the mind.

It is similarly unfortunate that the characters played by Hayden and Lancaster die relatively early in the story because these actors have the power needed to stand up to the film's other dominant elements. When they are around the quality of the finished product is noticeably improved; after they are gone the scenery and events take charge.

On reflection it can be suggested with some confidence that the main problems with *Novacento* are those of any artist when confronting a massive canvas after having served his apprenticeship on smaller works. The director's previous films had given him a comprehensive grounding in technique and showed a sound grasp of the essentials of human communication. In *Novacento* he falters when the human relationships, central to the core of his concept, fail to develop thoroughly and convincingly and are lost in the landscape.

Although he had become much less 'bankable' in his own country, Burt Lancaster was becoming an international presence and was regularly offered screen roles in Europe; but he was back on home ground for *Buffalo Bill and the Indians, or Sitting Bull's History Lesson* (1976).

The film picks a (presumably) deliberately uncertain path between reality and fiction. The Buffalo Bill (Paul Newman) who sits before us in old age is unreal, a character created by writer Ned Buntline (Lancaster). The old hunter-turned-showman no longer knows fact from fantasy. The old adage: 'When legend becomes fact, print the legend' has been transmuted into: 'Print the legend often enough and the fact will vanish forever.'

Any western buff entering this world of Buffalo Bill is in for a rude jolt, for although Paul Newman looks like the real (or is it the legendary?) man he is also a drunk with a memory so sodden it can no longer separate fact from fancy.

When Sitting Bull (Frank Kaquitts) gently undercuts the old showman's proud boasts with hints of reality he comes closest to being a figure with whom the audience can identify. Sadly, the Sitting Bull of the audience's preconception also bears little resemblance to reality.

The inability to differentiate between truth and fiction, allied to the significance of show business in America's conception of its past and present, provides director Robert Altman with his *raison d'être*.

It is a worthy cause, if only because Hollywood has been guilty of many and flagrant misuses of the nation's history in its fictional works. In particular, the legend of the Old West has been embroidered and fantasized beyond the point at which reality can hope to be reinstated. The generation now in charge of making films knows little of the past and what it does know has been grossly discoloured by the motion-picture industry. Inevitably, therefore, their audiences have a hard time knowing what to believe and what to discount.

Unfortunately for the overall impact of *Buffalo Bill and the Indians* (and along the way it has quite a number of visually commanding images), after seventy-odd years of film-making few people can avoid bringing to it a complex set of preconceptions which stem largely from what they have seen on other screens.

When the expectations these preconceptions generated were not met, audiences lost touch with their shaky historical foundations and were left disappointed, if not actually alienated.

Performances were mixed with John Considine and Geraldine Chaplin drawing some critical praise. In the central role, Paul Newman simply failed to connect with this strange and almost abstract vision of an American legend. Moving on the edges of the story, almost as a choric voice, Lancaster was given too little to do. Idle speculation, of course, but what kind of film might have resulted had Newman's and Lancaster's roles been reversed?

From the Old West of legend to a current event of marked if morbid public curiosity was where Lancaster went next. It was a step he might well have avoided making had he been given time to reflect. Unfortunately, *Victory at Entebbe* (1976) is a TV movie made in great haste to cash in on something which had recently occupied the world's headlines.

Lancaster, in the role of Israeli Minister of Defence Shimon Peres, is one of many stars featured in this account of the hijacking of an airliner which took refuge at Entebbe airport in Uganda and the subsequent spectacular commando raid by the Israeli army.

The nature of the real events had all the makings of high drama: intense political activity, personal tragedy, individual acts of heroism, stoic courage, and the sheer excitement of the commando raid. The makers of this and another opportunistic film must have thought that it couldn't miss – but it did.

The many commercial successes Lancaster had made over the years, most often with the good fortune of not having to compromise too much, had now placed him in a position where he could pick and choose his roles.

That being so, his remaining films of the 1970s should all have been artistically sound ventures. As *Victory at Entebbe* shows, this was not always the case and some of the ventures displayed a marked lack of judgement while others were clearly made just for the money. Nevertheless, running through many of them is a thread which suggests a line of liberal thought which may give some measure of the very private man beneath the actor's mask.

The private person had been even more deeply buried after his divorce from Norma. Television chat show appearances were rare and fraught with hazards for any unwary interviewer who strayed from previously agreed questions. Press interviews were tolerated as part of the business he was in, but were not encouraged.

As a result more than ever before details of Lancaster's private life often owed more to imaginative speculation than cold, hard, horse's-mouth facts. He could and did remain elusive and when he chose to talk in public the torrent of words told much of what went on in his mind but almost nothing of what moved in his heart.

Yet for all his reluctance to open up to others he would often agree to lecture to students on which occasions he would range widely – and wildly – over film acting and production, politics and world affairs, philosophy and religion.

When interviewed by John Doran in 1983 for Britain's Grampian Television, he was uncharacteristically loquacious as he talked about the actor's work. 'What is satisfactory for me, and I think for most actors, is to try to do something which seems ... a little beyond you ... stretches you, which enlarges your ... acting muscles and obviously it's more interesting than playing something you can walk through easily.'

In the light of such comments, it is hard to understand exactly what prompted him to lend his presence to *The Cassandra Crossing* (1977) which used the clichéd plot of placing a group of disparate characters in collective jeopardy and allowing them to solve personal crises while battling against some (usually arbitrary) outside danger.

Here, the characters are passengers on a train heading out of Geneva for Stockholm, unaware that one of their number is a terrorist who has become infected with a deadly man-made virus. Once the fact that the train is a speeding bacteriological time-bomb is known to governments along the route, panic sets in and the train is rerouted towards Poland where decontamination facilities exist at the site of a World War II concentration camp.

Buried beneath all its glossily packaged silliness, the film appears to carry some kind of message. Heavily pointed references to the Holocaust: sealed railway compartments, decontamination, a camp in Poland, and a diversion through Nuremberg, all imply a sense of purpose, but all is lost in the inanities of the script.

Apart from Lancaster, who plays the desk-bound Colonel Stephen Mackenzie whose job is to oversee the transfer of the train to a place where it can be destroyed, the passenger list includes Ava Gardner, Richard Harris (as a neurosurgeon who happens also to be an expert with machine-guns), Sophia Loren, Martin Sheen, and Lee Strasberg.

There was a sense of purpose in Lancaster's next film but this time the message was lost through interference by the producers who cut and distorted the director's work.

Twilight's Last Gleaming (1977) was based upon a straightforward action novel, Walter Wager's *Viper Three*. It ended up as pretty much the same sort of simple thriller even if director Robert Aldrich had striven to make much more of it.

The story concerns a former US Air Force officer, General Lawrence Dell (Lancaster), who has been unjustly imprisoned so that his criticism of the Vietnam war be silenced. The general breaks out of prison and seizes control of a Strategic Air Command missile silo in Montana which he helped design.

Dell threatens to fire off the silo's missile contingent unless the President of the United States, David T. Stevens (Charles Durning) agrees to pay a $10 million ransom, guarantees safe conduct out of the country, and broadcasts a secret National Security Council report on the conduct of the war in south-east Asia which will expose the real reasons for American involvement.

The president was unaware of this document (which reads in part: 'The objective of this war is to demonstrate to the Russians a brutal national will, that we have the willingness to inflict and suffer untold punishment. That no matter what the cost in American blood, we would perpetrate a theatrical holocaust'). He realizes its potentially damaging effect upon his administration. He orders General Martin Mackenzie (Richard Widmark), the man responsible for imprisoning Dell and who has convinced the president that Dell is bluffing, to attack and destroy the missile silo. So well built are these silos that the only way to wreck one is to detonate a small atomic device.

Mackenzie sends Armoured Personnel Carriers in a frontal assault which Dell watches through closed-circuit television cameras mounted atop one of the missile silos. (This film uses split-screen techniques and is one of the few occasions when this particular form of gimmickry works even if the method proves unsatisfactory when shown on television where some of the images are too small to be distinct.)

Dell responds to the attack with threats of his own and Mackenzie withdraws and the APCs are abandoned. However, all this activity has distracted Dell and his fellow escapees, Willie Powell and Augie Garvas (Paul Winfield and Burt Young), long enough for Mackenzie to put into effect his real plan. A helicopter descends directly over the television cameras, the installation's one blind spot, and lowers a team of men who are able to gain entry to the silo and set the atomic device.

Dell quickly proves Mackenzie's assumptions to have been dangerously false. He does have the means of launching the silo's nine Titan missiles when he instigates the countdown which he cancels at eight seconds to blast-off. There is no longer any room for manoeuvre; any move against Dell cannot hope to succeed in the eight seconds before nine Titans will be on their way towards Russia and the start of global destruction.

By now, despite strenuous opposition from his closest advisers, the president is considering meeting Dell's demand and telling the people the truth about Vietnam. The president agrees to accede to another of Dell's demands: that he will be hostage during the escape. Before leaving for Montana, the president elicits a promise from the ageing Secretary of Defense Zachariah Guthrie (Melvyn Douglas), that if he should be killed the NSC report will be broadcast.

Deep underground in the silo, the original two-man launch crew has tried fighting back and in the resulting mêlée a crewman and Garvas are killed.

Above ground, Mackenzie, now running the show from a control vehicle out of range of the silo's cameras, prepares for the final act. The abandoned APCs are not empty. Three sharpshooters lie in wait.

As Dell and Powell study the scene on their television monitors, the black criminal, freed by Dell from Death Row, displays a much clearer and more perceptive view of what is about to happen than does Dell. He even suspects the presence of the marksmen. The airforce man, for all his decisiveness in action, retains his establishment attitudes and beliefs. 'You think there are sharpshooters sitting out in those APCs?' Dell asks.

'They don't have to be in 'em', Powell replies. 'They could be under a rock or behind a blade of grass. Man, I had mere niggers in my outfit who could shoot the asshole out of a rat at a quarter of a mile. I mean, who knows, maybe they got a midget out there.'

'A what?'

'Some little bitty fellow we never even saw.'

Dell's 30 years of patriotic service are affronted and he draws himself up to his full height. 'There are no midgets in the United States Air Force,' he declares indignantly.

Powell is neither convinced nor intimidated. 'Fuck the Air Force, maybe they borrowed him from the Mafia. It's all the same company.'

As the president's aircraft arrives at the Montana base Powell cynically informs the general that they have taken on 'The Power' and there is no way they can win. Dell tells him that with President Stevens walking between them no one dare attack. Powell's cynicism explodes as he bitterly denounces Dell's blind trust in the establishment's adherence to democratic principles.

'You really are pitiful,' he snarls.

'What the hell are you trying to say?'

'I'm saying that they do not give a shit for the President of the United States. They will kill us all before they let that poor bastard make that speech on television. Don't you know they will never let him blow their gig. You declared war but they got the muscle. And they're gonna keep it, and Stevens is expendable.'

Powell's expectation is borne out when President Stevens becomes their hostage and the three men leave the silo. As they begin the long walk to a waiting aircraft, carefully circling to make a clear shot impossible, General Mackenzie hands responsibility for the final moves to the three marksmen.

Shots rattle out and all three fall. Dell and Powell are killed outright and the president is fatally wounded.

The sharpshooters stare in horror at what they have done; in his control vehicle Mackenzie turns from the television monitor in full realization that it is his head that will roll; further off, the president's advisers watch with remarkable detachment.

As President Stevens lies dying he calls for Guthrie. When the old man leans over him he repeats his earlier request that Guthrie must keep his promise to broadcast the contents of the NSC report on Vietnam. Guthrie refuses to repeat his promise and, looking into the old man's lizard eyes, the dying president knows that he has been betrayed.

Potentially, this film was strong stuff but most of director Aldrich's intentions were destroyed by weak-willed interference from producers. Much of the film's original political content was lost before release in America when almost half an hour was cut and little remained of the document that most exercises Dell and the president, and none of it is quoted. Thus, what remains after the cuts is virtually a non-political thriller (in Britain it appeared on the home video market retitled *Nuclear Countdown*).

Fortunaltely, when screened on British television in 1984 most of the missing scenes had been reinstated and the film thus recovered much of the depth, value and integrity that had gone into its making.

There are effective performances in all major roles with Durning especially good as the uneasy president. Lancaster gives a characteristic aura to the maverick general and in the restored version lends the film a powerful authenticity.

The initial loss of the message in *Twilight's Last Gleaming* must have been contagious because it happened again in *The Island of Dr Moreau* (1977). Based upon an H.G. Wells story already filmed as *Island of Lost Souls* (1932), this tale centres upon a doctor who has been dabbling with nature, turning animals into almost-men by altering their genes and carrying out appropriate surgery to tidy up loose eugenic ends. More often than not he has failed hopelessly and the results of these abortive experiments roam the jungle on two legs but with an interesting (if not very convincing) selection of animal heads on their shoulders.

H.G. Wells's story carried disturbing suggestions of man's potential ability to influence nature and to dictate his own future through genetic manipulation. The earlier film version (made when such possibilities were science-fiction dreams) sustains this message and packed quite a punch. Now that we know that science has already advanced far beyond Dr Moreau's messy antics the subject is much less acceptable in the form on display (in either film).

Setting aside the philosophical overtones, the film fails to convince, thrill or entertain and shows little sign of directorial authority. There are hints of last-minute rewrites: the beastmen profess a hatred of killing yet in the opening sequence one of two shipwrecked sailors is slaughtered. There may also have been budget problems, suggested by the fact that although for most of the film the beastmen number only a dozen or so, in the closing sequences scores more appear but keep in long shot where their make-up need not be too elaborate. And even those beastmen who do feature in close-ups look more like ordinary men wearing Halloween masks than the victims of genetic manipulation.

Philip Strick, in *Monthly Film Bulletin* (October 1977), was unhappy with the star's performance: 'It is hard to imagine that Burt Lancaster, at the best of times, could be an effective substitute for Charles Laughton; in place of decadent paranoia he provides a certain square-jawed zeal, but the essential sickness of Moreau evades him.'

This is a little unfair. In the light of recent scientific advances – and especially with the knowledge of what took place in Nazi concentration camps at the urging of real-life monsters such as Josef Mengele, August Hirt, Sigmund Rascher and their acolytes, zealotry may be closer to the mark than paranoia. The image Lancaster conveys, like that of the character he portrayed in *Judgement at Nuremberg*, chills because of his unquestioning black messianic fervour.

Lancaster was scheduled to appear in *The Wild Geese* when he learned of a project in which he felt he could make a personal statement on the Vietnam war. His interest in this other film was sufficient to help the production move forward from the talking stage but even so capital was hard to raise. In the end, Lancaster confirmed his commitment by putting $75,000 of his own into the project.

Unfortunately, audiences were rather thin for *Go Tell the Spartans* (1978), which is set in Vietnam in 1964, the time when the French army was pulling out to be replaced by American 'advisers'.

Commanding a group of Americans based at Penang is Major Asa Barker (Lancaster), an ageing veteran of too many wars. Vietnam is his third. Although a cool and able professional he is stuck at the rank of major following a serious breach of military etiquette which also happened to show a marked lack of plain commonsense. At a White House function he was enjoying fellatio, administered by his general's wife, when the general walked in accompanied by the President of the United States. As a result of this piece of sexual carelessness, Barker is doomed to serving out his days in the most foreign corners of his country's military field.

Ordered to scout the unoccupied village of Muc Wa, the major decides not to bother and sends in a phoney report. He isn't lazy or cowardly, he just doesn't believe that the village can serve any purpose to anyone, friend or foe. But his orders are repeated and this time the reluctant Barker sends out a platoon which is attacked along the way and has to dig in at the village.

Eventually, Barker flies into Muc Wa where, under orders now to abandon the village, he prepares to airlift himself and his fellow Americans out. Corporal Courcey (Craig Wasson) objects to the casual disregard for the friendly Vietnamese soldiers who are with them and for the frightened villagers who have begun to reappear in the surrounding jungle and insists on staying behind. When the dust from the rising helicopter settles Courcey sees that Barker has also stayed behind.

Barker and Courcey are very different kinds of men and make unlikely comrades-in-arms. Courcey is bright, intelligent and keen, and is consequently a total mystery to his cynically practical commander. Barker is in Vietnam because he's a professional soldier who goes where he is sent; that someone should volunteer for service in this dreadful place is beyond his comprehension.

Others in Barker's command are similarly disparate. Sergeant Oleonowski (Jonathan Goldsmith), who served with Barker in Korea, is tired and ready for rotation back home. When the fighting becomes too much for him, he ends his own life rather than go on with the ceaseless round of killing.

Lieutenant Hamilton (Joe Unger) is a new boy with as yet unsullied ideals of patriotism. Eventually, weakened with dysentery, Hamilton is killed but not before he has bewildered Barker with his Hollywood-inspired ideas of how warriors behave and speak. When he first reaches Muc Wa, Hamilton calls Barker on the radio and declares, 'We have met the enemy and they are ours'.

And then there is 'Cowboy' (Evan Kim), a Vietnamese who hates the Viet Cong with such homicidal intensity that he embarrasses the Americans who don't yet hate anybody.

With his depleted comrades and the villagers under his unwilling protection, Barker prepares to sneak out of Muc Wa at night but the peasants Courcey has befriended turn on the Americans and South Vietnamese. Everyone, old men, women and little children, attacks the Americans and Major Barker is mortally wounded.

When daylight comes, only Courcey remains alive. Around him lie the bodies of the dead, Barker's included, all ignominiously stripped of clothing. Sickened and dismayed, Courcey stumbles towards the French cemetery that stands on the edge of Muc Wa. A very old man appears and points a gun at him. Courcey ignores him, mumbling, 'I'm goin' home, I'm goin' home.' As the American staggers away, the old man collapses on the ground.

Above the entrance to the cemetery is the inscription, spoken by Simonides at Thermopylae, from which the film takes its title: 'Go tell the Spartans, thou who passest by, that here, obedient to their laws, we lie.'

Although *Go Tell the Spartans* falls short of the eventual stance Hollywood would take over Vietnam in such films as *Platoon* (1986) and *Full Metal Jacket* (1987), it is light years ahead of such jingoistic hokum as *The Green Berets* (1968). In that film John Wayne had heroically announced during a temporary retreat: 'We'll be back tomorrow ... God willin' ... and the river don't rise.'

There is no sign in *Go Tell the Spartans* of such false heroics. Here, the true manner of the passing of the many who died in Vietnam is eloquently portrayed in Barker's final moments. He settles back against the alien ground for which he is about to die and murmurs, 'Ah, shit.'

Fatalism pervades the film. As Peter McInerny commented in his article 'Apocalypse Then: Hollywood Looks at Vietnam' in the Winter 1979 issue of *Film Quarterly*: 'The story of Barker and the destruction of his command at Muc Wa dispassionately records circumstances and consequences without pretence, entangling us in a web of history and violence that trapped the best and brightest of an era.'

Go Tell the Spartans is clearer in its mind and purpose about the business of war than most Vietnam films made before the late 1980s. Inevitably, therefore, it is much more perceptive than almost all earlier films dealing with any one of a dozen wars. War is a sad, bitter and dirty business and if there is any implied lesson to be learned it comes partly from the repeated cry of most of the Americans in this film: 'It's *their* war.'

Intriguingly, *Go Tell the Spartans* also deliberately states the artificial attitude which many Americans brought to the Vietnam war. This attitude owed its origins to a generation brought up not on real war but on Hollywood's idea of war.

Briskly directed by Ted Post and with a gritty and realistic screenplay by Wendell Mayes, *Go Tell the Spartans* remains one of the better films to come out of that particular episode in recent American history.

Lancaster's performance is excellent, pitched with just the right amount of wry humour at his lot and displaying beneath the surface of his grizzled hard-bitten shell enough human warmth to show that whatever drove this man to become a professional soldier, a desire to inflict injury and death upon his fellow men was not a factor.

A different war on another continent provided the setting for Lancaster's next film. Once again it was a war fought for uncertain political motives on soil over which one of the historically favoured combatants had no rights but this time spectacle and dramatic action were the keynotes.

Zulu Dawn (1979) is set in nineteenth-century Africa and sets out to examine events leading up to those depicted in the 1963 film *Zulu*.

Unlike its notable predecessor, *Zulu Dawn* is not helped by the fragmentary nature of its story-line. Whereas *Zulu* told the tightly contained story of the fate of British soldiers at Rorke's Drift (which took place a few hours after the events described in the new film), *Zulu Dawn* cross cuts between different elements of the story.

The spectacle of the fighting is well executed but again there is not the impact of the earlier film. Like the earlier film, *Zulu Dawn* is replete with famous faces but the episodic story-line leaves inadequate time for building characterizations and the audience is hard-pressed to care what happens to individuals.

For all such difficulties, some good performances emerge from the principals who include Denholm Elliott, John Mills and Peter O'Toole.

Lancaster serves king and country in a suitably proud manner but like the others he is limited in what he can do with his role. Nevertheless, his solid, determined and impeccably honest presence gives weight to the character of Colonel Anthony

Durnford, a man doomed to losing his life through the stupidity of inferior men who happen also to be his superior officers.

Almost contemporary with *Zulu Dawn*, but several thousand miles away in space and a long way further in ambience, was the setting for Lancaster's next film.

Cattle Annie and Little Britches (1979) is set in the American West and tells the ostensibly true story of Annie McDougal and her friend Jennie Stevens.

In real life the girls grew tired of being poor but honest and in 1893 became camp-followers of the notorious Doolin-Dalton outlaw gang. Annie was then seventeen years old and cheerfully offered her tender young body in fair exchange for free booze and some excitement in the Oklahoma Territory. Her friend Jennie was two years younger but had similarly few compunctions about exchanging sex for some of life's little comforts.

In 1894 US Marshal Big Bill Tilghman set his sights on Bill Doolin and in the course of arresting the outlaw also picked up Cattle Annie and Jennie (known as Little Britches from her habit of wearing men's clothing, when she was wearing anything at all). Doolin was imprisoned to await trial but escaped to New Mexico then, riskily, came back to Oklahoma to settle down. He was a sick man, however, and in 1896 he died of consumption. (Soon after Doolin's death, US Marshal Heck Thomas appeared on the scene and promptly fired both barrels of his shotgun into the still-warm corpse, and claimed the $5,000 reward which he handed over to the outlaw's widow.)

Big Bill Tilghman handed in his badge in 1914 and supervised the making of an early motion picture, *The Passing of the Oklahoma Outlaws*. In 1924, then aged seventy, Tilghman pinned on the tin star again as peace officer of a booming oil town. He was shot dead by a government agent in league with local bootleggers. The jury, showing respect neither for age, transient fame nor history, found the lawman's killer 'Not Guilty'.

The film version of some of these events (which are, naturally enough, clouded in the mists of legend) stays close enough to the truth in most respects but isn't so slavish as to impugn the purity of the two young ladies. Cattle Annie and Little Britches (Amanda Plummer and Diane Lane) are bright-spirited creatures who appear to have a fairly chaste relationship with

Bill Doolin (Lancaster) who isn't really as old as he appears here. He is a legend, however, and that as much as anything is what fascinates the girls. Seeing the outlaws in a much more romantic light than that in which the outlaws see themselves, the girls persuade the gang to sharpen up their image.

Although the legend becomes the fact for a while, as the smartened-up outlaws indulge in a rash of law-breaking, fate and the inexorable passage of time catch up with them.

The messenger of fate is Marshal Tilghman (Rod Steiger) who is also old and legendary (the real Big Bill was only forty years old when these events took place) and just as handy with a gun as the outlaws he hunts.

A preoccupation of Hollywood westerns since 1960 has been the relationship between old comrades and even former enemies who can see that time is passing them by. These often uncomfortable companions accordingly find solace in each other's company even if they sometimes glare at one another over the barrels of their guns.

This extension of the 'buddies' theme so popular in American film and literature offers interesting opportunities to examine issues from opposing moral standpoints. Many of the resulting westerns missed the opportunity completely while some made a reasonable stab at it. Among the latter were Lancaster's teaming with Gary Cooper in *Vera Cruz*, another the Robert Mitchum-George Kennedy film, *The Good Guys and the Bad Guys* (1969). Only a very tiny number fully realized the possibilities. Ranking high among those that did is Sam Peckinpah's *Ride the High Country* (1962) with Joel McCrae and Randolph Scott. (This film is a rare example of a change of title for the British market improving upon the original: *Guns in the Afternoon* suitably evokes the potent atmosphere of this classic.)

Perhaps *Cattle Annie and Little Britches* doesn't quite hit the high mark of Peckinpah's film, and neither does it have the resonance of the Mitchum-Kennedy effort, but it is far better than many of its kind and deserved better than the manner in which it was slid almost apologetically on to the market.

Performances are pretty much as expected when two skilled old stagers work together. As Derek Elley commented in *Films and Filming* (June 1980), 'the playing of Lancaster and Steiger is beautifully shaded, Lancaster especially good as the ageing outlaw with life in him yet, gently philosophizing over the impermanence of his profession and the needs which drove him to assume it.'

All in all, *Cattle Annie and Little Britches*, while no earth shaker, was a pleasant way in which to end the 1970s, a decade which had provided Lancaster with something of a mixed bag of roles.

Even his most ardent fan would have admitted that some of the gloss of his earlier film roles had faded and as the decade came to a close he could have been forgiven had he decided to retire. He was sixty-six years old and had already made more than that number of films. He was rich by any standards and he could look back on a career of great success as an actor and as a producer. True, his production companies had faded, but largely as a result of financial difficulties generated by his steadfast refusal to put commercial criteria ahead of consideration of artistic merit.

In his private life his relationship with Jackie Bone had given him a new stability; he lived well and travelled extensively; and as much as ever enjoyed his beloved opera (he was on the board of the Los Angeles opera). His children were all active in one or another branch of the arts although only one, William, writer of the Walter Matthau hit comedy *The Bad News Bears*, is in the motion-picture business.

But he still wanted to act. Unfortunately, the parts he was being offered were far beneath the standard he had reached after all the years he had spent perfecting his craft.

Allen Eyles, writing in *Movies of the Fifties*, commented: 'If recently Lancaster has not found the right parts to suit a performer of his advancing years, he remains an actor who cares about the work he does and the meaning it has, and is unusually conscientious about the responsibilities of screen stardom.'

For all the accuracy of this summation, at the start of the 1980s it looked as if Burt Lancaster was doomed to fade quietly into obscurity. But then, against all the odds, he landed a part which was not only perfect for him but was one which allowed him to bring into one film the distillation of all that he had learned in thirty-three years in the business.

8 International Hero

Early in 1980 Burt Lancaster was hospitalized for surgery. Although rapidly-scotched rumours had suggested something worse, he had gall bladder trouble which necessitated a lengthy operation and a brief spell on the critical list. More serious medical problems lay ahead but for now he swiftly recovered and was soon back at work.

The past few years had seen Lancaster's box-office appeal diminishing. The reasons for this lay chiefly in the changing nature of cinema audiences; his long-standing fans no longer went to the cinema in sufficient numbers while the new generation of moviegoers had other heroes.

As for the character roles that had filled his middle years, these were now fewer and further between – at least those of any real quality.

He may have given up hope of finding a part worthy of his consummate talents but miracles sometimes happen – even in Hollywood.

It is rare to find a film about which only superlatives will suffice and which has no discernible weaknesses in any facet of its construction, but *Atlantic City* (1981) is such a film.

From its opening moments to the final fade-out not a single false note is struck and repeated viewings bring not boredom but awareness of still more fine touches of the film-maker's art.

The story centres upon a small group of social misfits in Atlantic City where, as the town is turned into a pale, cold imitation of Las Vegas, the past is forced to give way to the present.

Lou Pascal (Lancaster) is an ageing numbers runner. A leftover from the glory days before World War II, Lou lives in a crumbling apartment building on the boardwalk, a short

143

distance from where glittering new casinos are springing up. One floor below lives Grace (Kate Reid), another relic of a bygone age. Back in the 1940s Grace came to Atlantic City to take part in a Betty Grable lookalike contest, stayed behind and married. Long widowed and now mostly bedridden, she is cared for by Lou who was a friend of her late husband.

In the apartment across the way from Lou's lives Sally (Susan Sarandon), a waitress at an oyster bar in one of the casinos. In the hope of improving her status in life, Sally – like Lou a born loser – is training to become a croupier.

Into town comes Sally's husband, Dave (Robert Joy), who ran away some time back with her sister. Sally is coerced into accommodating Dave and her heavily pregnant sister, Chrissie (Hollis McLaren), until they can find a place of their own. As much as she dislikes the greasy Dave, Sally still feels protective towards her not-too-bright sister but is unaware that in Philadelphia Dave intercepted a cocaine drop.

As Dave begins looking for a buyer for the drugs he meets Lou who helps him make a contact for the first sale. But two emissaries from the drug dealers in Philly are hard on Dave's heels and kill him, leaving Lou with four thousand dollars in his pocket and most of the cocaine still hidden in his apartment.

With money to burn after years of scraping by, Lou smartens himself up with new clothes and entertains Sally. His recovered confidence in himself allows him to tell her how, at night, he watches as she stands in her window rubbing lemon juice on to her arms and shoulders and breasts (which she does to rid herself of the smell of shellfish). The old man and the young woman become lovers but Lou's illusions of a return to his high-rolling past (which exists mostly in his imagination) are rudely shattered when Dave's killers turn up and savagely beat Sally while he stands by, helpless and afraid.

Lou starts to trade the remaining cocaine to a bemused dealer (who first mistakes him for a collector for Medicare) and soon builds a pile of cash. When Sally is fired from the casino for associating with criminals, Lou persuades her to leave town with him and head for Florida.

As they prepare to leave the two heavies stop them but this time Lou is armed and he kills them both. Elated at having finally lived up to a reputation that exists only in his mind, Lou and Sally take the car belonging to the dead men and drive to a motel on their way towards a future together.

During the night Lou cannot make love to Sally and in the small hours of the morning, unable to sleep, he takes the telephone into the bathroom to call Grace and boast of his exploits.

Unaware that Lou is watching her from the bathroom, Sally takes most of Lou's money and when he returns to the bedroom announces that she is going out to buy breakfast for them both. He offers to go but she insists and he hands her the keys to the car. As she leaves the motel room Lou quietly tells her not to keep the car too long but to ditch it at the first opportunity.

In the final sequence, Grace, on her feet for the first time, calls on Lou's customer with another delivery of cocaine. Having collected another thousand dollars, Grace walks unsteadily along the corridor to where Lou waits. Arm in arm, the two old people walk off together.

Atlantic City is filled with references, visual and aural, to past, present and future. Almost the first sight is the dynamiting of a stately old building which will make way for a blank-faced steel-and-granite structure. Everywhere, men are working, some tearing down old buildings while others erect new ones. The sound of jack-hammers constantly reverberates through the city.

The red plushy interior of Grace's apartment is an oasis in the middle of the bleak, echoing apartment building that will soon end as a pile of rubble.

As Lou makes his daily bet-collecting round he is impervious, or tries to be, to the fact that many of his old customers are winning more money on the casino slot machines than he has ever paid out in all his years in the numbers racket.

The impression of the past as a better place is fixed superbly in one masterly line of dialogue which is nonsense and yet makes perfect sense. Walking along the boardwalk with the egregious Dave, Lou reminisces over the past and observes: 'Tutti frutti ice cream and craps don't mix. The Atlantic Ocean was something then. Yes, you should've seen the Atlantic Ocean in those days.'

Contrasts of different sorts abound. As Sally identifies the body of her brutally murdered husband she can hear Robert Goulet, hired to open the Frank Sinatra Wing at the local hospital, singing an inane song extolling the virtues of Atlantic City.

Music is used extensively to underline change and to enhance characterization. In Grace's apartment, the music playing on an old phonograph is Tommy Dorsey's 1940s hit, 'Song of India', while in the casinos rock bands rattle out current hit-parade material. And wherever Sally goes she has a miniature cassette player on which she listens to 'Casta Diva' from Bellini's *Norma*, part of her vain attempt to improve herself.

The blending of the characters' dreams and their eventual realization that this is all that they are is handled with deep sensitivity by director Louis Male working from a faultless screenplay by John Guare.

Every role is superbly played. Among the minor, yet fully-rounded parts, are the elderly lavatory attendant Lou knows from the old days and the vastly-amused poker player to whom Lou sells his cocaine.

The supporting roles of Dave and Chrissie are made to look and sound just right while Kate Reid's performance as Grace is a delight.

The two principals play their roles to perfection. Susan Sarandon portrays Sally as a young woman who is not quite bright enough nor quite pretty enough to make the big-time she fondly imagines is just around the corner. She avoids pathos, while showing in every moment of her round and pain-filled eyes that she is doomed to be one of life's losers.

As Lou, the small-time hoodlum with dreams he never truly hopes to fulfil, Burt Lancaster achieves the summit of a career filled with fine performances. His pathetic cringing as Sally is beaten up before his eyes is transformed when Grace berates him for his ineffectualness and impotency. When she demands to know if he's really a man, he yells down the stairs, 'I'm a *lover*.'

Lou's acceptance of Sally's reverence when he shows that he knows how to order wine; the unpatronizing conversation with his old friend the lavatory attendant when he gives him his old suit; his elation at the moment of the killing of the two hoods; the resignation when he acknowledges that he and Sally cannot hope to have a joint future – all are just a few of many marvellous moments in the film.

Perhaps best of all is the close-up of his eyes as he looks from between the slats of the window-blind at the girl rubbing lemon juice on to her naked breasts in the opposite window. The eyes convey not sick lust but a kind of dignified sadness that his sexuality has been so pathetically reduced.

It could have surprised no one that Lancaster was nominated for awards for this role. He won Best Actor Award from the New York Film Critics Circle, the Los Angeles Film Critics Association, and the British Academy of Film and Television Arts (for the ceremony he wore a battered blue lounge suit – the smartest thing he'd worn in years – and still attracted more attention than those in immaculate dress suits).

He failed to win the Oscar, that award going to Henry Fonda (for *On Golden Pond*) just a few weeks before his death in what was widely regarded as a sympathy vote. Lancaster was sanguine about the result, remarking, 'I'm glad he got it … it was a wonderful performance.'

As the years pass, *Atlantic City* must be seen as worthy of more than the relatively transient glory such awards bring. It is nothing less than a triumph of all facets of cinematic art and of the art of screen acting in particular.

In August 1981, Lancaster returned briefly to the stage when he appeared in San Francisco with Kirk Douglas. This was in *The Boys of Autumn* in which an ageing Huck Finn and Tom Sawyer meet again and reminisce over their lives. Lancaster played Huck to Douglas's leading role of Tom, a decision reached on the flip of a coin.

Although they both enjoyed the experience they also found it hard work.

For Lancaster, the next move was back to Italy and more films. Unfortunately, unlike many of his Italian projects, *La Pelle* (*The Skin*, 1981) was somewhat misconceived. Lancaster played World War II General Mark Clark in a film which, while star-studded (he co-starred with Claudia Cardinale and top-billed Marcello Mastroianni), lacked the glow of originality and the qualities displayed by his other films in Italy. Indeed, reviews of the film slammed its clogged story-line which crammed in as much as possible just so long as good taste was no criterion.

Also in Italy, and similarly anti-climactic, was a ten-hour epic made for television in which Lancaster played the role of Pope Gregory X. This was *Marco Polo* (1982) wherein he shared cameo screentime with many other notable names including John Gielgud and Anne Bancroft. Very popular when screened in its country of origin, this mini-series failed to receive international distribution despite its multinational cast.

From the boardwalk of Atlantic City by way of the Vatican to a remote corner of the Scottish Highlands might seem a wilfully capricious journey. Certainly, at first glance Lancaster's next role appears to have been a whimsically lightweight choice. In the event, his decision to play a role in *Local Hero* (1983) was most felicitous.

Written and directed by Bill Forsyth, *Local Hero* recounts events in a tiny Scottish fishing village which becomes the target of a massive and immensely rich American oil company.

Knox Oil and Gas Corporation wants land on which to build a huge oil terminal and has chosen the bay which shelters the village of Ferness. Felix Happer (Lancaster), the chairman of Knox, is a dreamer; he never wanted to run an oil company and all his spare time is spent staring into the sky through a telescope pursuing his one great love – astronomy.

When Happer visits Ferness – attracted by reports that the aurora borealis is lighting up the sky – he takes over negotiations for the purchase of the land which, by this time, means talking the one villager with no interest in money, old Ben Knox (Fulton Mackay), into selling. From Ben the oil tycoon learns that there is nothing the old man wants. Indeed, the opposite might be the case for Ben has much that Happer envies, not least of which is his contentment in knowing what really matters in life.

Additionally, Happer learns that not only do he and Ben share a passion for astronomy but that it was Ben's father who founded Knox Oil. When Knox Sr sold out to Happer's father the two sons, Ben and Felix, were set on courses through life which were very different to what might have been.

Happer decides to abandon thoughts of building an oil refinery; instead he will build an observatory.

Fully realized from Bill Forsyth's original conception (he had even thought of Lancaster in the role of Felix Happer while the script was still in embryo stage), *Local Hero* has about it all the gentle charm of the Ealing comedies to which it has sometimes been unfairly compared since it has much more sophistication and a greater wholeness.

All the main roles are well portrayed with almost equal credit deserved throughout. The many inexperienced actors clearly benefited from working with older hands and the film can certainly be likened to the Ealing films in the sense of teamwork which abounds in every scene.

For Lancaster, appearing in *Local Hero* might seem to have been an eccentric whim in keeping with the film's galaxy of such characters; but, as he pointed out, he no longer needed to work and could please himself by playing only those roles which appealed to him for their intrinsic merits.

From his choices of the early 1980s few could find fault with that philosophy. As to finding understanding of his attitude, which allowed him to take the roles of Lou Pascal and Felix Happer, so apparently out of keeping with his popular image yet so absolutely right in the event, perhaps his own words are best used. 'As you get older you have to keep your mind open. I feel you must also try new things. Some of us learn finally that maturity means consideration for other people. I think it is the ability to love yourself and consequently others. That is the answer. I know now that it is not necessary to go through life being a warrior.'

The most eagerly awaited aspect of Lancaster's next film was the fact that it marked the return to film-making after six years of director Sam Peckinpah. For Lancaster, *The Osterman Weekend* (1983) was a return to the half-world of the CIA. Unlike *Scorpio*, however, where he was an agent ruthlessly revenging himself upon his murderous and unprincipled boss, here he is the boss inflicting misery upon one of his agents.

Lawrence Fassett (John Hurt) is an unstable individual who believes that his wife was murdered by the combined efforts of the CIA and the KGB under the guidance of CIA Director Maxwell Danforth (Lancaster). In his efforts to find the men directly responsible for killing his wife, Fassett accidentally unearths a clandestine organization known as Omega. He tells Danforth that this is a spy-ring consisting of three well-heeled Californians: Bernard Osterman (Craig T. Nelson), Joseph Cardone (Chris Sarandon) and Richard Tremayne (Dennis

Hopper). Unconnected with Omega but friendly with all three men is John Tanner (Rutger Hauer), a television journalist specializing in exposés.

Fassett persuades Danforth that they should let the ring continue to function while trying to turn one of the trio into a double-agent. With Tanner's assistance Fassett sets up a weekend party at the TV man's home which he fills with cameras and assorted electronic gadgetry. Complications arise when an attempt is made to kidnap Tanner's wife Al (Meg Foster) and their young son. The Omega men panic and, with Tanner distraught, events spiral out of control. Tremayne, Cardone and their wives are blown up and Osterman and Tanner are threatened by the increasingly unstable Fassett.

Eventually, Fassett, who has now himself kidnapped Tanner's wife and child, is able to confront Danforth (remotely through a television link-up). By now it is clear that Omega is not a spy-ring but an elaborate currency swindle. Fassett has rigged evidence to force Danforth into the open and admit his part in arranging the death of Fassett's wife. Tanner, meanwhile, has turned the tables on Fassett and his electronic wizardry by tracking him down whilst apparently still appearing live on television. Tanner shoots Fassett in the process of rescuing his wife and child.

The Osterman Weekend is ultimately unsatisfactory in its complex interweaving of TV and video gimmickry (already in 1983 the least imaginative of contemporary film-making clichés) and the seldom believable motivation of the main character. Sadly, Peckinpah's death at Christmas 1984 abruptly ended his briefly renewed career.

There is much that is creditable in the film, not least solid performances by all the leading players. Yet there is a lingering suspicion that many of the complications of the plot are there just to fill in time and could have been eliminated without damaging the structure of the film. The mind turns naturally to *Scorpio* and the simple and straightforward manner in which agent Lancaster disposes of CIA Director McLeod. *The Osterman Weekend* could have benefited from some of its gun-in-a-paper-bag bluntness.

Lancaster's enjoyment of opera made him a natural host for a 1983 Italian television series *The Life of Verdi* (which starred

Ronald Pickup as the composer), but that same year he was admitted to Cedars of Lebanon–Mount Sinai Hospital in Los Angeles for tests.

Doctors decided that quadruple bypass surgery was necessary and Lancaster promptly set about building up his strength. His spirited decision to overlook the fact that he was seventy paid off when, after more than five hours on the operating table, he recovered rapidly, was out of bed in a couple of days and out of hospital in ten.

Despite the speed of his recovery, several of Lancaster's projected film roles had to be taken over by others. In *Firestarter* (1984) he was replaced by Martin Sheen while in *Maria's Lovers* (1984) Robert Mitchum stepped into the breach. A less likely role he gave up was that taken by William Hurt in *Kiss of the Spider Woman* (1984), and James Mason substituted for him in *A.D.* (1985).

If he had ever needed an excuse to stop working he had one now. In fact the reverse happened and after a false start he began a remarkably sustained period of work – mostly small roles in American films and starring roles in Europe.

The false start came in the summer of 1984 when he travelled to Spain where he hoped to start work on *Le Marchand des Quatre Saisons*, written and to be directed by Chilean-born Miguel Littin. Financial problems hit this production at the last minute and after a couple of weeks in the sun, Lancaster packed his bags and went home.

Those few days relaxing in sunny Spain proved to be the last holiday he would have for quite some time.

9   Life Goes On

Between his September 1983 heart surgery and his return to filming in 1984, Burt Lancaster celebrated his seventieth birthday.

Despite the extraordinary confidence with which he had begun his film career thirty-four years earlier, he can scarcely have expected it to have gone on so long and at such a high level of international recognition.

That he had been so phenomenally successful, and remained so despite changing tastes among audiences, can be accounted for chiefly by his abiding desire to hone and polish his craft and his determination wherever possible to work in quality films. That these were not always critical and box-office winners was rarely something for which he had been responsible. Indeed, in the films in which he appeared in his seventies he was often the best thing on view in what were otherwise misconceived or inadequate productions.

If some of the films in which he appeared were less than distinguished it was never because Lancaster's perception of them was unfocused. In a 1972 interview with the *Guardian*'s Derek Malcolm he had commented upon the ineptness of many screenwriters, insisting that in all his years in the business he had read only two scripts which, in first draft, were of any distinction: *Birdman of Alcatraz* and *Ulzana's Raid*. Doubtless he would have later added *Atlantic City* to this brief catalogue but it seems unlikely that many of the other new scripts of the 1980s met his high standards in first draft, if only because the version of the scripts which appeared in the finished article often left much to be desired.

In *Little Treasure* (1985) Lancaster has the best part in a film which uneasily blends a story of the reuniting of an old man and his daughter with a routine thriller. By the end of the first reel, the family tale has given way to the thriller and Lancaster's character is dead. The fact that the first reel is also the best part of the film conveys much about the strength of Lancaster's portrayal and the inability of the film's makers to make better use of the material in their hands.

Margo Teschemacher (Margot Kidder) arrives in a seedy little town in Mexico where her father now lives. He has sent for her, enclosing with his letter a bus ticket and a promise of a legacy. Along with Eugene Wilson (Ted Danson), a man she met on the bus, Margot drives out to find that her father's 'estate' is a broken down hut in the middle of nowhere.

Her father, Delbert Teschemacher (Lancaster) had deserted Margo and her mother many years ago and now lives a grubby existence cared for only by Evangelina (Melena Doria), a Mexican woman. The old man tells Margo that many years before he had participated in a bank robbery and now plans to take her – his 'little treasure' – on a spending spree with the remaining loot. But before he can recover the money Teschemacher dies from a heart attack brought on when an untreated injury develops gangrene.

With her father dead, Margo and Eugene, who have begun an affair, set out to find the money knowing only that it is buried in a ghost town somewhere in New Mexico.

After many trials and not a few tribulations, among which is Margo's decision to take a job as a stripper to enable her to survive, Margo and Eugene finally recover her father's buried treasure.

Before its release *Little Treasure* was likened to *The Treasure of the Sierra Madre* which suggests that the film's publicists allowed their occupational delusions to blind them to reality. Even the first half hour isn't that good and once Lancaster's character is dead and buried the rest is mostly aimless drifting with just a few hints that in other hands – and in another film – a story about Margo alone might have been a better idea.

Another film which was heralded with hints of past glories is *Scandal Sheet* (1985) in which Lancaster returned to the world of sleaze journalism he had last visited in *Sweet Smell of Success*. Likening this film to that earlier success was generally unjustified although the setting was generally similar.

Helen Grant (Pamela Reed) is a forceful and highly successful freelance journalist whose services are sought by Harold Fallen (Lancaster). Fallen is owner of *Inside World*, a newspaper which exists on the need of millions to read salacious gossip about showbiz personalities. With neither the readers nor the writers of these stories caring much if they are true or false, Fallen and his people pry under stones and through keyholes to get the dirt on their targets.

The reason Fallen makes Helen an offer she cannot refuse is that she is a friend of film stars Ben Rowan and Meg North (Robert Urich and Lauren Hutton). Fallen is determined to destroy Rowan's attempts to rescue his career which is suffering as a result of his alcoholism, and Helen inadvertantly allows herself to be used in such a way that Rowan kills himself. Shattered by what has happened, Helen tries to explain herself to Meg North but is rejected just as her attempts to return to 'legitimate' journalism are frustrated because no one will hire her now that she has been tainted through her association with Fallen.

In the end, Helen settles for the fact that she is what she has become – another of Fallen's vultures.

Although suffering somewhat from the needs of American television both in the way it looks and in how even the most villainous characters have redeeming features, *Scandal Sheet* has the virtue of avoiding a cop-out ending. Solid performances from Grant, Hutton, Urich and Max Wright as Stan Clark, the egregious journalist who shows Helen the slimy ropes of her new trade enhance the film.

Lancaster's performance is unusual. In the scenes set in his office – a glass-sided box in the middle of an open space which gives him the appearance of a spider at the centre of his web – he dominates easily just by being there. His scenes with Pamela Reed are less certain because he seems simply too nice to be what he is supposed to be.

He does, however, sport an interesting line in clothes which change progressively through the film, as if outwardly defining his nature. Starting from comfortable tweeds he graduates to plain dark business suit and finally appears in black suit, shirt and hat, all set off with a white tie, rather like a reincarnated Chicago hoodlum from the 1930s.

On Wings of Eagles (1986), another television venture, was based upon real events in Iran in 1979 which were novelized by Ken Follett. When two Americans were imprisoned in Tehran it fell to a band of ex-army civilians to get them out.

Hired by H. Ross Perot (Richard Crenna) Colonel Arthur D. 'Bull' Simons (Lancaster) plans a daring and ultimately successful rescue venture. Although a little wordy in its early 'setting up' stages (it occupies five hours of TV time), *On Wings of Eagles* is mostly a crisp old-fashioned action film in which the good guys come out on top. Lancaster clearly revelled in his role and gained good reviews although the generally poor results of America's other real-life interventions in Iran might well have given commentators a slightly rose-coloured view of this particular and unusually victorious encounter.

The Burt Lancaster–Kirk Douglas double act had had its most recent airing at the 1985 Academy Award ceremonies and seemed like a gold-plated certainty at the box-office if only the right vehicle could be found.

Tough Guys (1986) certainly looked like being the right vehicle and was, in the event, an interesting near miss. Unfortunately for further reunions, box-office results were rather less than brilliant.

Released from prison after serving thirty years apiece for their part in committing the last train robbery in America, Harry Doyle and Archie Long (Lancaster and Douglas) immediately find themselves the targets of an equally ageing hitman Leon B. Little (Eli Wallach). Also on their trail is Deke Yablonski (Charles Durning), the lawman who sent them to prison and who is convinced they will again take to crime.

Obliged under the terms of their parole to separate, Harry and Archie try to fit into their new surroundings: Harry in an old people's home where his humiliation is softened by the presence of old flame Belle (Alexis Smith); Archie in one menial job after another.

Eventually the pair decide to return to crime and set their sights on the 'Gold Coast Flyer', the train they robbed thirty years ago and which is about to make its final run. Aided by Little, who was merely attempting to fulfil an old contract on Harry and Archie, and Dana Carvey (Richie Evans), their parole officer, the tough guys board the train and put their plan into effect. Despite the efforts of Yablonski to foil them they succeed, running the train off its rails over the desert and across the border into Mexico.

It is all improbable stuff but might have been memorable had the film's makers avoided the obvious and made a little more of the effect of freedom on two men who hadn't seen the outside of prison in half a lifetime.

Lancaster and Douglas play well together and Lancaster is also good in his scenes with Alexis Smith. There is also good support from Durning and Wallach but the energy of these superannuated heroes (who really did the train-top scenes without benefit of stuntmen) deserved rather better from both script (written with them in mind) and direction which hints at nervousness. This last point is understandable, given that in the past both leads have been known to eat directors before breakfast, but *Tough Guys* suffers as a result.

For all the glamour of Lancaster's first career in the circus he was allowed only rarely to re-enter that world on the screen. The role of flamboyant showman Phineas Taylor Barnum was made to measure for him and in *Barnum* (1986) he leaped at the opportunity to play this fast-talking extrovert who created 'the Greatest Show on Earth' which became an integral part of nineteenth-century American show business.

Lancaster's dynamic portrayal of Barnum as an engaging, forceful combination of con man and promoter, artist and impresario helped bring the film rather more accolades than are usually granted to television movies of the week.

Lancaster's next role was also for television but was a very different affair. Made in Germany, *Sins of the Fathers* (1986) told a tale based loosely upon the industrial dynasty of the I.G. Farben family. Lancaster plays the role of Carl Julius Deutz who builds his business as a manufacturer of chemicals for peaceful uses. Only later does his son-in-law, Heinrich Beck (Bruno Ganz), redirect the enterprise into unacceptable areas with the manufacture of poisonous gas and chemicals for mass extermination.

Strongly cast with mainly German supporting players but also with Julie Christie as Deutz's daughter, *Sins of the Fathers* (entitled *Fathers and Sons* when screened in Britain) tells an intriguing tale of family loves and jealousies during a period of German history which eventually reshaped the world.

Although it was also set in Germany, Lancaster's next film was made in Italy for cable television. *Control* (1987) uses as its premise an investigation into the psychological effect of nuclear war on people.

Madame Havemeyer (Ingrid Thulin) is head of a corporation which has designed a nuclear fallout shelter and, wishing it to be tested, calls in retired nuclear scientist Herbert Monroe (Lancaster). Among the fifteen people sent into the shelter for the test are Mike Zella (Ben Gazzara) Sarah Howell (Kate Nelligan) and Camille Dupont (Kate Reid). While there they are unwittingly subjected to a scheme of Monroe's which overrides that of the builders of the shelter.

Monroe devises a means of convincing his guinea-pigs that nuclear war really has broken out which thus allows him to put those in the shelter to what he sees as a much more meaningful test.

Despite the underlying gravity of purpose, *Control* is basically a variation on the old people-in-jeopardy story to which film-makers regularly turn. Well-written, directed and performed though it is, the film eventually becomes a fairly predictable exercise. This is unfortunate because, coming as it did so soon after Chernobyl had reawakened temporarily dormant fears, it could have had much to say about the world in which we live and will die.

While in Italy, Lancaster also made a brief appearance as a cardinal in *The Betrothed* (1987), a film which failed to obtain wide release elsewhere.

In 1987 he also made an appearance in *The Jeweller's Shop*, a film which despite its origins had a hard time attracting international attention from distributors. Based upon a story by Andrzej Jawien, *The Jeweller's Shop* is an unusual view of love. The story traces the lives of two couples, Stefan and Anna (Ben Cross and Jo Champa) and Andrej and Teresa (Andrea Occhipinti and Olivia Hussey) who meet and marry in Cracow, Poland, in 1939. They buy their wedding rings from a jeweller's shop where the mystical owner (Lancaster) explains to them the significance of their actions and the rings which will bind them together even after death.

After the war Stefan and Anna live in Canada with their daughter Monica and there they are joined by the widowed

Teresa and her son. Years later, as the children grow up they fall in love but Monica (Melora Hardin), aware of the failings of her parents' life together believes that marriage to Chris (Jonathan Crombie) can lead only to unhappiness.

Then Anna tried to sell her wedding ring but the jeweller to whom she takes it – and who resembles the old man in the shop in Cracow – persuades her to try again with her marriage. She does so and this convinces Monica that she should change her mind and marry Chris.

Simplistic in its view of human relationships, especially those between men and women, the story gained much of its worldwide popularity through its playwright's eventual rise to become Pope John Paul II.

Lancaster was impressed enough with the story, however, commenting as much during press conferences held to promote the film which nevertheless failed to reach the audience its makers doubtless expected.

Although he had successfully avoided the dangers of typecasting in his early years in the business, Lancaster was now in danger of being typed as a dessicated survivor of past glories. He had done this magnificently in *Atlantic City* and with notably less success in *Little Treasure* and *Tough Guys*. Now came another variation on the theme.

While looking good on paper, *Rocket Gibraltar* (1988) rather missed its potential. Levi Rockwell (Lancaster) is approaching his seventy-seventh birthday and his family gather around him for the celebrations. Rockwell is no ordinary man; in his life he has been a writer of distinction and such radicalism as to have been blacklisted. A poet, teacher by vocation, Rockwell loves the sea which borders his Long Island estate. Reconciled to his imminent death – something of which his children and grandchildren are not at first aware – Rockwell provides a rock-like centre to the lives of all those who live in his shadow.

Although often uneasy in its presentation – the old man and one of his grandchildren appear to communicate telepathically – and in its assumptions about the meaning of life, *Rocket Gibraltar* had a difficult time while still in production at Columbia (where David Puttnam was briefly making waves). Among the changes made were in the film's director with Daniel Petrie taking over from Amos Poe, the former underground film-maker.

The basic premise of self-centred adults unable to communicate with anyone, least of all their own children and parents who are thus driven to form a bond which straddles the middle generation, and who only recognize their failings when forced to confront the death of their patriarch is one which film-makers seem to love. Certainly, it is a theme to which they regularly turn even if it is one which bears little resemblance to the lives of the average audience.

Here, the way of life of Rockwell's son and one of his three daughters is far from ordinary and hence not too readily understandable. Rollo (John Glover) is a movie producer glued to his portable telephone as if his life depends upon it, and Aggie (Suzy Amis) is determined to sleep with just about every man she meets. With his other daughters married to a failed baseball-player and a has-been comic, not surprisingly the old man prefers to spend his time telling tall tales to the next generation.

They, in response, take one of his tales literally and when he dies try to give him an exit appropriate to a Viking warrior by casting him adrift on his burning boat, the *Rocket Gibraltar*.

Off screen, Burt Lancaster continued to show his liberal sympathies with television comments in support of ACLU which had been subjected to attacks by presidential candidate George Bush. He also showed anger at being passed over for the starring role in *Old Gringo* (which went instead to Gregory Peck) because the film's makers were unable to obtain insurance following Lancaster's heart surgery. Lancaster's response to this rejection was a $1.5 million lawsuit, his estimate of his loss of earnings from the project.

On a happier note, he appeared with the California Chamber Virtuosi at the Smothers Theatre, Pepperdine University, San Francisco for a performance of Saint-Saens's 'Carnival of the Animals' in which he read Ogden Nash's verses.

Film offers continued to arrive in his mail. Perhaps it was inevitable that many film-makers were influenced by those same insurance needs that torpedoed his projected appearance in *Old Gringo* and most of the offers were for small roles.

At best this was unfair and an unrealistic assessment of his physical capacity. His record since his 1983 heart operation showed that no one need have lost too much sleep over any imagined inability to complete a film. He had taken leading roles in *Little Treasure, Scandal Sheet, On Wings of Eagles, Tough Guys, Barnum* and *Rocket Gibraltar*. None of these was a makeweight role and two (Harry Doyle in *Tough Guys* and Phineas T. Barnum) were demandingly energetic.

Nevertheless, small role offers abounded and once in a while he chose to take advantage of such moments and his appearance as the ghostly Dr 'Moonlight' Graham in *Field of Dreams* (1989) was a deftly engaging example.

Obscurely, for their financial commitments are no less than those of theatrical film-makers, the majority of the leading roles of recent years had come from television.

It was for television that he made *Phantom of the Opera* (1990), the latest in a long line of screen versions of Gaston Leroux's tale of a hideously disfigured individual living in the bowels of the Paris Opera House. In this version, Erik (Charles Dance), the masked Phantom, lurks in ornate splendour beside an almost silvan lagoon far beneath the streets of the city, living only for the sounds of beautiful music that waft downwards to where he hides. His fear of contact with his fellow men lies in the fact that he was born badly disfigured. Up above, the opera's managing director, Gérard Carrière (Lancaster) is replaced by the upstart Cholet (Ian Richardson) who promptly instals his paramour, Carlotta (Andrea Ferreol), as prima donna. Meanwhile, a young woman with a fine but untrained voice arrives in Paris. She is Christine Daée (Teri Polo) who has been sent there for 'training' by Count Philippe de Chagny (Adam Storke) whose love for a well-turned soprano has led him to people the opera's chorus with his trainees.

Erik hears Christine's voice, is captivated and comes up to meet her and offer to teach her. Needless to say, he falls in love with her; equally needless to add, the young count is similarly besotted. Eventually, Christine insists on seeing Erik's face but faints away with shock at what is revealed, thus sending the Phantom into terminal decline.

When Carrière comes to aid Erik he reveals that he is the Phantom's father. Christine, too, wants to help but is encouraged by the rascally Cholet who brings in the police (anxious to talk to the Phantom who had earlier dropped a chandelier on to an audience unkind enough to boo Christine off stage). After a roof-top struggle, Erik is beseeched by Christine to save the life of the Count but the police close in, intent on taking him alive. Erik silently implores his father to save him from this fate by the only means possible; Carrière shoots his son who lingers just long enough for Christine to come to his side, remove his mask, and kiss him.

Leroux's original novel was rampantly melodramatic and most film versions have followed the path he signposted. This one doesn't even try for melodrama and, indeed, falls uncomfortably between two stools. The Erik-Christine-Count triangle is played as a straightforward if simple-minded love story. Similarly straight is the relationship between Erik and his father, even if this is brought in only in the last quarter of the tale. On the other hand, Cholet and Carlotta play their scenes as if for farce but it is all so heavy-handed that these passages succeed only in falling flat.

Despite the experience of writer and director, the whole thing moves turgidly and there is none of the expected tension. Even the revelation to Christine of Erik's disfigurement is kept from the audience who never catch a glimpse of the face that launched a dozen remakes.

Performances are variable with some rather atrocious dubbing making the actors sound almost as bad as they are sometimes made to appear. Lancaster's role is apparently an addition as Erik's father had not featured in previous versions and he does what he can with his scenes; indeed, he brings a measure of sensitivity to the scenes he shares with Erik towards the end of the film.

Interviewed about his role, Lancaster commented that he enjoyed making *Phantom of the Opera* for the chance to hear the operatic excerpts (sung by members of the Hungarian State Opera) and these performances certainly help break the tedium of this overlong film. Unfortunately, it isn't enough and, all things considered, this particular Phantom would have been best left in the sewers beneath the city.

Late 1989, when *Phantom of the Opera* was being made also brought news of another television mini-series; this one, entitled *Saga*, was planned to co-star him with Charlotte Rampling and Rutger Hauer.

Also in 1989 he received a television offer of a somewhat

different kind and in December, shortly after his seventy-sixth birthday, travelled to Britain to work again with Bill Forsyth who had directed him in *Local Hero*. (On this visit Lancaster was accompanied by Susan Scherer, his relationship with Jackie Bone having ended some time earlier.)

The result of this visit appeared on British television screens in the early summer of 1990: two 70-second, half million pound advertisements for Foster's lager. Commenting on his roles in these, Lancaster remarked on how he had been attracted by the fact that, unlike the hard-sell commercials to which he was accustomed back home, these came in the form of little stories. He was also happy to work again with Forsyth, observing that if he got into trouble he was sure the director would help him out.

Coincidentally (well, probably), a season of his films was screened on the independent network. Then, in early December 1990, news came that serious illness had struck Lancaster again, when he was visiting a friend in hospital. Although not immediately confirmed, it emerged that the star had suffered a stroke. Once more, this seemingly indestructible actor's life was in the balance.

Thus, as 1991 dawned, it proved impossible to speculate upon what the future might hold for Burt Lancaster. But, if this tough-minded and physically powerful individual could have his way, there seems little doubt that the last chapter in a long, demanding and enormously successful career is yet to be written.

Afterword

Assessing any actor's role in film history is always difficult. A glance at those films in which leading players have been replaced by others as a result of illness, injury or death and which have, nevertheless, turned out well clearly demonstrates that nobody is indispensable.

For all that, Burt Lancaster's career is lavishly sprinkled with film appearances of a very special kind and had he not made them the chances are the alternative versions would have been inferior.

Even his first role, as Ole Andreson in *The Killers*, carried with it a special quality few of the other *film noir* heroes of the day could have matched. His Captain Vallo, in *The Crimson Pirate*, was a magnificent exercise in old-time swashbuckling that bears comparison with Fairbanks and Flynn at their best. The title role in four films of the 1960s gave him an opportunity to vividly display all facets of his superb technical command: *Elmer Gantry*, *Birdman of Alcatraz*, *The Leopard*, and *The Swimmer*.

Additional to his acting roles, of course, were his achievements as a producer of commercially improbable films like *Marty*.

But it is as an actor that he is best remembered and he was able to bring impressive undercurrents to a string of what might otherwise have been routine westerns, of which *Ulzana's Raid* is but one example. His committed venture into the sometimes murky waters of Hollywood's interest in the Vietnam war, *Go Tell the Spartans*, was similarly underscored with great depths. And late in his career he brought to *Barnum* a splendidly vital performance as an over-the-top con man. Then, of course, there is his role as Lou Pascal in *Atlantic City*, a performance of sheer perfection in a similarly flawless film.

Had Burt Lancaster appeared in only these ten films – indeed, had he made only the last of those named – his place in Hollywood's history would be assured. But, of course, what he did in these roles cannot be viewed in isolation. Everything he did intertwines with everything else. Throughout the years since 1946 he has constantly learned and developed and demonstrated an abiding interest in his craft.

There were some who, early in his career, were blinded to the variety and depths of his talent. Indeed, Lancaster himself helped cloud the view of others with occasionally dismissive remarks such as: 'The only style I have is as Burt Lancaster does'. The majority of observers of the film scene eventually came around however and today few writers on film argue against Lancaster's place as a major star who also happens to be a major talent.

Certainly there can be few filmgoers who would deny that without Burt Lancaster the motion-picture business would be less than it is.

Lancaster's own view of his work is not always easy to nail down. While he has never been as dismissive as, say, Robert Mitchum, one of his contemporaries, he seldom opens up. On those odd occasions when he does decide to talk, however, he does so vividly and extensively even if, at the end, he concedes that the business he has been in for the past forty-plus years depends not on words but pictures.

In his 1983 television interview with John Doran he mused on film as a medium, commenting:

> I don't know how much good it really does in the long run but I think that as far as the morality of the world is concerned, in terms of the way we're living now, a good film does have something to say to people ... it's a constant reminder that there has to be a moral structure of the whole world to which we adhere ... or the whole thing [will] go to pieces.
>
> So a good film ... a meaningful film, a film that really has something to say is ... very important and very effective. More than people just telling it in words.

Fortunately for audiences, many of Burt Lancaster's films have been good and meaningful and have had something to say. Because of this, they will live on long after he has gone from the scene.

As for those latter-day actors who might strive to take his place, it is hard to see any among those who fill the screens of 1990s cinemas who have the ability to master the breadth of his range.

Put another way, they don't make 'em like Burt Lancaster any more.

Bibliography

Adair, Gilbert, *Hollywood's Vietnam* (Proteus, London, 1981)

Cody, Iron Eyes & Perry Collin, *Iron Eyes* (Muller, London, 1982)

Fury, David, *The Cinema History of Burt Lancaster* (Artist's Press, Minneapolis, 1989)

Gow, Gordon, *Hollywood in the Fifties* (A.S. Barnes, New York, 1971)

Hunter, Allan, *Burt Lancaster: The Man And His Movies* (Paul Harris, Edinburgh, 1984)

Lloyd, Anne & David Robinson, (eds.), *Movies of the Fifties* (Orbis, London, 1982)

McLoughlin, Dennis, *The Encyclopedia of the Old West* (Routledge & Kegan Paul, London, 1977)

Robinson, Edward G., *All My Yesterdays* (W.H. Allen, London, 1974)

Silver, Alain & Elizabeth Ward, (eds.), *Film Noir* (Secker & Warburg, London, 1980)

Thomas, Bob, *Brando* (W.H. Allen, London, 1973)

Wallis, Hal B. & Charles Higham, *Starmaker* (Macmillan, London, 1980)

Windeler, Robert, *Burt Lancaster* (W.H. Allen, London, 1984)

Winters, Shelley, *Shelley, Also Known As Shirley* (Granada, London, 1981)

Filmography

As all film buffs know, the delay between the end of production and a film's release can vary from a few months to some years. In the following schedule of Burt Lancaster's film roles (which includes his appearances in television films but not his work on TV documentaries) release dates have been used. This filmography therefore follows the same sequence as used in the main text.

Details have been culled from a number of sources including the films themselves, studio publicity, the BFI's *Monthly Film Bulletin*, and *Variety*.

THE KILLERS (1946)
U-I (Mark Hellinger)   105 minutes
Director: Robert Siodmak   Photographer: Woody Bredell
                                       (b&w)
Screenplay: Anthony Veiller (from Ernest Hemingway's short story)
Music: Miklos Rozsa
Leading players: Burt Lancaster, Edmond O'Brien, Ava Gardner, Albert Dekker, Sam Levene, Charles McGraw, William Conrad

VARIETY GIRL (1947)
Paramount (Daniel Dare)   93 minutes
Director: George Marshall   Photographers: Lionel Lindon,
                                       Stuart Thompson (b&w)
Screenplay: Edmund Hartmann, Frank Tashlin, Monte Brice, Robert Welch
Leading players: Mary Hatcher, Olga San Juan, De Forrest Kelley with cameos by Burt Lancaster, Gary Cooper, Alan Ladd, Bob Hope

BRUTE FORCE (1947)
U-I (Mark Hellinger)   98 minutes
Director: Jules Dassin   Photographer: William Daniels
                                       (b&w)

Screenplay: Richard Brooks
Music: Miklos Rozsa

Leading players: Burt Lancaster, Hume Cronyn, Charles Bickford, Yvonne De Carlo, Ann Blythe, Sam Levene, Charles McGraw

DESERT FURY (1947)
Paramount (Hal B. Wallis)   96 minutes
Director: Lewis Allen   Photographers: Charles Lang,
                                   Edward Cronjager (Technicolor)
Screenplay: Robert Rossen
Music: Miklos Rozsa
Leading players: Burt Lancaster, Lizabeth Scott, Wendell Corey, John Hodiak, Mary Astor

I WALK ALONE (1948)
Paramount (Hal B. Wallis)   98 minutes
Director: Byron Haskin   Photographer: Leo Tover (b&w)
Screenplay: Charles Schnee from Theodore Reeves's play *Beggars are Coming to Town*
Music: Victor Young
Leading players: Burt Lancaster, Kirk Douglas, Lizabeth Scott, Wendell Corey, Marc Lawrence, Mike Mazurki

ALL MY SONS (1948)
U-I (Chester Erskine)   94 minutes
Director: Irving Reis   Photographer: Russell Metty
                                   (b&w)
Screenplay: Chester Erskine from Arthur Miller's play
Music: Leith Stevens
Leading players: Burt Lancaster, Edward G. Robinson, Howard Duff, Mady Christians

SORRY, WRONG NUMBER (1948)
Paramount (Hal B. Wallis, Anatole 89 minutes
Litvak)
Director: Anatole Litvak   Photographer: Sol Polito (b&w)
Screenplay: Lucille Fletcher from her own radio play
Music: Franz Waxman
Leading players: Burt Lancaster, Barbara Stanwyck, Wendell Corey, Ann Richards, Ed Begley

KISS THE BLOOD OFF MY HANDS (UK TITLE: BLOOD ON MY HANDS) (1948)
Universal/Norma (Harold Hecht)   79 minutes
Director: Norman Foster   Photographer: Russell Metty
                                   (b&w)
Screenplay: Leonardo Bercovici from Gerald Butler's novel
Music: Miklos Rozsa
Leading players: Burt Lancaster, Joan Fontaine, Robert Newton

CRISS CROSS (1949)

U-I (Michael Kraike)   87 minutes
Director: Robert Siodmak   Photographer: Franz Planer
                                         (b&w)
Screenplay: Daniel Fuchs from Don Tracy's novel
Music: Miklos Rozsa
Leading players: Burt Lancaster, Yvonne De Carlo, Dan Duryea,
Stephen McNally (bit part by Tony Curtis in début role)

ROPE OF SAND (1949)

Paramount (Hal B. Wallis)   105 minutes
Director: William Dieterle   Photographer: Charles Lang
                                         (b&w)
Screenplay: Walter Doniger
Music: Franz Waxman
Leading players: Burt Lancaster, Paul Henreid, Claude Rains, Peter
Lorre, Corrine Calvet

THE FLAME AND THE ARROW (1950)

Warner (Harold Hecht, Frank   88 minutes
Ross)
Director: Jacques Tourneur   Photographer: Ernest Haller
                                         (Technicolor)
Screenplay: Waldo Salt
Music: Max Steiner
Leading players: Burt Lancaster, Virginia Mayo, Robert Douglas, Frank
Allenby, Nick Cravat

MR 800 (1950)

TCF (Julian Blaustein)   90 minutes
Director: Edmund Goulding   Photographer: Joseph La Shelle
                                         (b&w)
Screenplay: Robert Riskin from an article by St Clair McKelway
Music: Sol Kaplan
Leading players: Burt Lancaster, Edmund Gwenn, Dorothy McGuire,
Millard Mitchell

VENGEANCE VALLEY (1951)

MGM (Nicholas Nayfack)   83 minutes
Director: Richard Thorpe   Photographer: George Folsey
                                         (Technicolor)
Screenplay: Irving Ravetch from Luke Short's novel
Music: Rudolph G. Kopp
Leading players: Burt Lancaster, Robert Walker, Joanne Dru, Ray
Collins, John Ireland

JIM THORPE, ALL-AMERICAN (UK TITLE: MAN OF BRONZE) (1951)

Warner (Everett Freeman)   107 minutes
Director: Michael Curtiz   Photographer: Ernest Haller
             (b&w)
Screenplay: Douglas Morrow, Everett Freeman
Music: Max Steiner
Leading players: Burt Lancaster, Charles Bickford, Steve Cochran, Phyllis Thaxter

TEN TALL MEN (1951)

Columbia/Norma (Harold Hecht) 97 minutes
Director: Willis Goldbeck   Photographer: William Snyder
             (Technicolor)
Screenplay: Roland Kibbee, Frank Davis
Music: David Buttolph
Leading players: Burt Lancaster, Gilbert Roland, Keiron Moore, John Dehner, Mike Mazurki

THE CRIMSON PIRATE (1952)

Warner/Norma (Harold Hecht) 104 minutes
Director: Robert Siodmak   Photographer: Otto Heller
             (Technicolor)
Screenplay: Roland Kibbee
Music: William Alwyn
Leading players: Burt Lancaster, Nick Cravat, Torin Thatcher, James Hayter, Noel Purcell, Eva Bartok

COME BACK, LITTLE SHEBA (1952)

Paramount (Hal B. Wallis) 99 minutes
Director: Daniel Mann   Photographer: James Wong Howe
             (b&w)
Screenplay: Ketti Frings from William Inge's play
Music: Franz Waxman
Leading players: Burt Lancaster, Shirley Booth, Terry Moore, Richard Jaeckel

SOUTH SEA WOMAN (1953)

Warner (Sam Bischoff)   89 minutes
Director: Arthur Lubin   Photographer: Ted McCord
             (b&w)
Screenplay: Edwin Blum from William M. Rankin's play
Music: David Buttolph
Leading players: Burt Lancaster, Virginia Mayo, Chuck Connors

THREE SAILORS AND A GIRL (1953)

Warner (Sammy Cahn) 95 minutes
Director: Roy Del Ruth Photographer: Carl Guthrie
(Technicolor)
Screenplay: Roland Kibbee, Deverey Freeman from George S.
Kaufmann's play *The Butter and Egg Man*
Music: Sammy Fain, Sammy Cahn
Leading players: Jane Powell, Gordon MacRae, Gene Nelson with guest
appearance by Burt Lancaster

FROM HERE TO ETERNITY (1953)

Columbia (Buddy Adler) 118 minutes
Director: Fred Zinnemann Photographer: Burnett Guffey
(b&w)
Screenplay: Dalton Trumbo from James Jones's novel
Music: George Duning
Leading players: Burt Lancaster, Deborah Kerr, Montgomery Clift,
Frank Sinatra, Donna Reed, Ernest Borgnine

HIS MAJESTY O'KEEFE (1954)

Warner/Norma (Harold Hecht) 92 minutes
Director: Byron Haskin Photographer: Otto Heller
(Technicolor)
Screenplay: Borden Chase, James Hill
Music: Robert Farnon
Leading players: Burt Lancaster, Joan Rice, Andre Morell, Abraham
Sofaer

APACHE (1954)

UA/Hecht-Lancaster (Harold 91 minutes
Hecht)
Director: Robert Aldrich Photographer: Ernst Laszlo
(Technicolor)
Screenplay: James R. Webb from Paul I. Wellman's novel *Bronco Apache*
Music: David Raksin
Leading players: Burt Lancaster, Jean Peters, John McIntire

VERA CRUZ (1954)

UA/Hecht-Lancaster (James Hill) 94 minutes
Director: Robert Aldrich Photographer: Ernest Laszlo
(Superscope & Technicolor)
Screenplay: Roland Kibbee, James R. Webb, Borden Chase
Music: Hugo Friedhofer
Leading players: Burt Lancaster, Gary Cooper, George Macready,
Cesar Romero, Ernest Borgnine

THE KENTUCKIAN (1955)
UA/Hecht-Lancaster (Harold Hecht)   104 minutes
Director: Burt Lancaster   Photographer: Ernest Laszlo (Technicolor)
Screenplay: A.B. Guthrie from Felix Holt's novel *The Gabriel Horn*
Music: Bernard Herrmann
Leading players: Burt Lancaster, Diana Lynn, Dianne Foster, Walter Matthau

THE ROSE TATTOO (1955)
Paramount (Hal. B. Wallis)   117 minutes
Director: Daniel Mann   Photographer: James Wong Howe (b&w)
Screenplay: Tennessee Williams from his own play
Music: Alex North
Leading players: Burt Lancaster, Anna Magnani, Marisa Pavan, Virginia Grey

TRAPEZE (1956)
UA/Hecht-Lancaster (James Hill)   105 minutes
Director: Carol Reed   Photographer: Robert Krasker (CinemaScope & De Luxe Color)
Screenplay: James R. Webb from Max Catto's novel *The Killing Frost*
Music: Malcolm Arnold
Leading players: Burt Lancaster, Tony Curtis, Gina Lollobrigida, Thomas Gomez, Katy Jurado

THE RAINMAKER (1956)
Paramount (Paul Nathan, Hal. B. Wallis)   121 minutes
Director: Joseph Anthony   Photographer: Charles Lang (VistaVision & Technicolor)
Screenplay: N. Richard Nash from his own play
Music: Alex North
Leading players: Burt Lancaster, Katharine Hepburn, Wendell Corey, Lloyd Bridges

GUNFIGHT AT THE OK CORRAL (1957)
Paramount (Hal B. Wallis)   122 minutes
Director: John Sturges   Photographer: Charles Lang (VistaVision & Technicolor)
Screenplay: Leon Uris
Music: Dimitri Tiomkin
Leading players: Burt Lancaster, Kirk Douglas, John Ireland, Frank Faylen, Jo Van Fleet, Rhonda Fleming

SWEET SMELL OF SUCCESS (1957)

UA/Norma-Curtleigh (James Hill)   96 minutes
Director: Alexander MacKendrick   Photographer: James Wong Howe
                                    (b&w)
Screenplay: Ernest Lehman, Clifford Odets from Lehman's short story
'Tell Me About It Tomorrow'
Music: Elmer Bernstein
Leading players: Burt Lancaster, Tony Curtis, Susan Harrison, Martin
Milner, Sam Levene, Emile Meyer

RUN SILENT, RUN DEEP (1958)

UA/Hecht-Hill-Lancaster (William   93 minutes
Schorr)
Director: Robert Wise   Photographer: Russell Harlan
                                    (b&w)
Screenplay: John Gay from Edward L. Beach's novel
Music: Franz Waxman
Leading players: Burt Lancaster, Clark Gable, Jack Warden, Brad
Dexter, Nick Cravat

SEPARATE TABLES (1958)

UA/Hecht-Hill-Lancaster (Harold   98 minutes
Hecht)
Director: Delbert Mann   Photographer: Charles Lang
                                    (b&w)
Screenplay: John Gay, Terence Rattigan from Rattigan's play
Music: David Raksin
Leading players: Burt Lancaster, Rita Hayworth, David Niven, Wendy
Hiller, Deborah Kerr

THE DEVIL'S DISCIPLE (1959)

UA/Hecht-Hill-Lancaster/   82 minutes
Brynaprod (Harold Hecht)
Director: Guy Hamilton   Photographer: Jack Hildyard
                                    (b&w)
Screenplay: John Dighton, Roland Kibbee from George Bernard Shaw's
play
Music: Richard Rodney Bennett
Leading players: Burt Lancaster, Kirk Douglas, Laurence Olivier

THE UNFORGIVEN (1960)

UA/Hecht-Hill-Lancaster/James   125 minutes
(James Hill)
Director: John Huston   Photographer: Franz Planer
                                    (Panavision & Technicolor)
Screenplay: Ben Maddow from Alan le May's novel *The Siege at Dancing
Bear*
Music: Dimitri Tiomkin

Leading players: Burt Lancaster, Audrey Hepburn, Audie Murphy, Charles Bickford, Lillian Gish, Doug McClure

ELMER GANTRY (1960)

UA (Bernard Smith)	146 minutes
Director: Richard Brooks	Photographer: John Alton (Eastmancolor)

Screenplay: Richard Brooks from Sinclair Lewis's novel
Music: André Previn
Leading players: Burt Lancaster, Jean Simmons, Arthur Kennedy, Shirley Jones, Dean Jagger

THE YOUNG SAVAGES (1961)

UA/Contemporary (Pat Duggan)	103 minutes
Director: John Frankenheimer	Photographer: Lionel Lindon (b&w)

Screenplay: Edward Anhalt, J.P. Miller from Evan Hunter's novel *A Matter of Conviction*
Music: David Amram
Leading players: Burt Lancaster, Shelley Winters, Dina Merrill, Telly Savalas

JUDGEMENT AT NUREMBERG (1961)

UA/Roxlom (Stanley Kramer)	190 minutes
Director: Stanley Kramer	Photographer: Ernest Laszlo (b&w)

Screenplay: Abby Mann from his own television play
Music: Ernest Gold
Leading players: Burt Lancaster, Spencer Tracy, Richard Widmark, Maximilian Schell, Montgomery Clift, Judy Garland, Marlene Dietrich

BIRDMAN OF ALCATRAZ (1962)

UA/Hecht-Lancaster (Stuart Miller, Guy Trosper)	148 minutes
Director: John Frankenheimer	Photographer: Burnett Guffey (b&w)

Screenplay: Guy Trosper from Thomas E. Gaddis's book
Music: Elmer Bernstein
Leading players: Burt Lancaster, Telly Savalas, Karl Malden, Thelma Ritter, Edmond O'Brien

A CHILD IS WAITING (1963)

UA (Stanley Kramer)	104 minutes
Director: John Cassavetes	Photographer: Joseph La Shelle (b&w)

Screenplay: Abby Mann
Music: Ernest Gold
Leading players: Burt Lancaster, Judy Garland, Bruce Ritchey, Gena Rowlands

THE LIST OF ADRIAN MESSENGER (1963)

U-I/Joel (Edward Lewis) 98 minutes
Director: John Huston Photographer: Joe MacDonald
    (b&w)
Screenplay: Anthony Veiller from Philip MacDonald's novel
Music: Jerry Goldsmith
Leading players: George C. Scott, Dana Wynter, Clive Brook with guest
appearances by Burt Lancaster, Tony Curtis, Robert Mitchum, Frank
Sinatra, Kirk Douglas

THE LEOPARD (IL GATTOPARDO) (1963)

TCF/Titanus/Pathe Cinema/SGC 205 minutes
(Goffredo Lombardo)
Director: Luchino Visconti Photographer: Giuseppe Rotunno
    (Technirama & Technicolor)
Screenplay: Luchino Visconti, Suso Cecchi d'Amico, Pasquale Festa
Campanile, Enrico Medioli, Massino Franciosa from the novel by
Giuseppe Tomasi di Lampedusa
Music: Nino Rota
Leading players: Burt Lancaster, Claudia Cardinale, Alain Delon, Paolo
Stoppa, Serge Reggiani, Romelo Valli

SEVEN DAYS IN MAY (1964)

Seven Arts/Joel (Edward Lewis) 120 minutes
Director: John Frankenheimer Photographer: Ellsworth
    Fredericke (b&w)
Screenplay: Rod Serling from the novel by Fletcher Knebel and Charles
W. Bailey II
Music: Jerry Goldsmith
Leading players: Burt Lancaster, Kirk Douglas, Fredric March,
Edmond O'Brien, Martin Balsam, Ava Gardner

THE TRAIN (1964)

UA/Ariana/Dear (Jules Bricken) 140 minutes
Directors: John Frankenheimer, Photographer: Jean Tournier,
Arthur Penn Walter Wottitz (b&w)
Screenplay: Franklin Coen, Frank Davis, Walter Bernstein from Ross
Valland's book *Le Front de l'Art*
Music: Maurice Jarre
Leading players: Burt Lancaster, Paul Scofield, Jeanne Moreau

THE HALLELUJAH TRAIL (1965)

UA/Mirisch/Kappa 167 minutes
Director: John Sturges Photographer: Robert Surtees
    (Ultra Panavision 70 & Technicolor)
Screenplay: John Gay from Bill Gulick's novel
Music: Elmer Bernstein

Leading players: Burt Lancaster, Lee Remick, Brian Keith, Donald
Pleasance, Martin Landau, Jim Hutton

THE PROFESSIONALS (1966)

Columbia/Pax (Richard Brooks)   123 minutes
Director: Richard Brooks   Photographer: Conrad Hall
                                      (Panavision & Technicolor)
Screenplay: Richard Brooks from Frank O'Rourke's novel *A Mule for the
Marquesa*
Music: Maurice Jarre
Leading players: Burt Lancaster, Lee Marvin, Robert Ryan, Jack
Palance, Woody Strode, Claudia Cardinale

THE SCALPHUNTERS (1968)

UA/Bristol/Norlan (Jules Levy,   102 minutes
Arthur Gardner, Arnold Laven)
Director: Sydney Pollack   Photographers: Duke Callaghan,
                                      Richard Moore (Panavision & De
                                      Luxe Color)
Screenplay: William Norton
Music: Elmer Bernstein
Leading players: Burt Lancaster, Ossie Davis, Telly Savalas, Shelley
Winters

THE SWIMMER (1968)

Columbia (Frank Perry, Roger   94 minutes
Lewis)
Director: Frank Perry   Photographer: David L. Quaid
                                      (Technicolor)
Screenplay: Eleanor Perry from John Cheever's short story
Music: Marvin Hamlisch
Leading players: Burt Lancaster, Kim Hunter, Janice Rule, Diana
Muldaur, Cornelia Otis Skinner, Marge Champion

CASTLE KEEP (1969)

Columbia (Martin Ransohoff,   107 minutes
John Calley)
Director: Sydney Pollack   Photographer: Henri Decae
Screenplay: Daniel Taradash, David Rayfiel from William Eastlake's
novel
Music: Michel Legrand
Leading players: Burt Lancaster, Peter Falk, Jean-Pierre Aumont,
Patrick O'Neil, Tony Bill, Bruce Dern

THE GYPSY MOTHS (1969)

MGM (Hal Lander, Bobby Roberts)

110 minutes

Director: John Frankenheimer

Photographer: Philip Lathrop (Metrocolor); Aerial photographer; Carl Boenisch

Screenplay: William Hanley from James Drought's novel
Music: Elmer Bernstein
Leading players: Burt Lancaster, Deborah Kerr, Gene Hackman

AIRPORT (1970)

Universal/Ross Hunter (Jacques Mapes)

136 minutes

Director: George Seaton

Photographer: Ernest Laszlo (Todd-AO & Technicolor)

Screenplay: George Seaton from Arthur Hailey's novel
Music: Alfred Newman
Leading players: Burt Lancaster, Dean Martin, Jean Seberg, Van Heflin, George Kennedy, Helen Hayes

LAWMAN (1971)

UA/Scimitar (Michael Winner)

99 minutes

Director: Michael Winner

Photographer: Robert Paynter (Technicolor)

Screenplay: Gerald Wilson
Music: Jerry Fielding
Leading players: Burt Lancaster, Lee J. Cobb, Robert Ryan, Robert Duvall, Sheree North, J.D. Cannon

VALDEZ IS COMING (1971)

UA/Norlan (Ira Steiner)

90 minutes

Director: Edwin Sherin

Photographer: Gabor Pogany (De Luxe Color)

Screenplay: Roland Kibbee, David Rayfiel
Music: Charles Gross
Leading players: Burt Lancaster, Susan Clark, John Cypher, Richard Jordan

ULZANA'S RAID (1972)

Universal (Robert Aldrich)

103 minutes

Director: Robert Aldrich

Photographer: Joseph Biroc (Technicolor)

Screenplay: Alan Sharp
Music: Frank De Vol
Leading players: Burt Lancaster, Bruce Davison, Jorge Luke, Richard Jaeckel, Lloyd Bochner

SCORPIO (1973)
UA/Scimitar (Walter Mirisch)   114 minutes
Director: Michael Winner   Photographer: Robert Paynter
                                      (Technicolor)
Screenplay: David W. Rintels, Gerald Wilson
Music: Jerry Fielding
Leading players: Burt Lancaster, Paul Scofield, J.D. Cannon, John
Colicos, Alain Delon, Gayle Hunnicutt

EXECUTIVE ACTION (1973)
Wakefield Orloff (Edward Lewis)   91 minutes
Director: David Miller   Photographer: Robert Steadman
                                      (colour)
Screenplay: Dalton Trumbo from a story by Mark Lane and Donald
Freed
Music: Randy Edelman
Leading players: Burt Lancaster, Robert Ryan, Will Geer, John
Anderson

THE MIDNIGHT MAN (1974)
Universal/Norlan (Roland Kibbee,   117 minutes
Burt Lancaster)
Directors: Roland Kibbee, Burt   Photographer: Jack Priestley
Lancaster   (Technicolor)
Screenplay: Roland Kibbee, Burt Lancaster from David Anthony's
novel *The Midnight Lady and the Mourning Man*
Music: Dave Grusin
Leading players: Burt Lancaster, Susan Clark, Cameron Mitchell,
Morgan Woodward

CONVERSATION PIECE (1975)
Rusconi/Gaumont/International   122 minutes
(Giovanni Bertolucci)
Director: Luchino Visconti   Photographer: Pasqualino de
                                     Santis (Technicolor)
Screenplay: Luchino Visconti, Suso Cecchi d'Amico, Enrico Medioli
Music: Franco Mannino
Leading players: Burt Lancaster, Silvana Mangano, Helmut Berger,
Claudia Marsani

MOSES (1976)
RAI/ITC (Vincenzo Labella)   141 minutes (originally 6 × 50
                                     minute episodes)
Director: Gianfranco de Bosio   Photographer: Marcello Gatti
                                     (colour)
Screenplay: Anthony Burgess, Vittorio Bonicelli
Music: Ennio Morricone
Leading players: Burt Lancaster, Anthony Quayle, Ingrid Thulin, Irene
Papas

NOVACENTO (UK & USA TITLE: 1900) (1976)

TCP/PEA (Alberto Grimaldi) 245 minutes
Director: Bernardo Bertolucci Photographer: Vittorio Storaro
  (Technicolor)
Screenplay: Bernardo Bertolucci, Franco Arcalli, Giuseppe Bertolucci
Music: Ennio Morricone
Leading players: Burt Lancaster, Sterling Hayden, Robert De Niro,
Gerard Depardieu, Donald Sutherland

BUFFALO BILL AND THE INDIANS, OR SITTING BULL'S HISTORY LESSON (1976)

UA (Robert Altman) 125 minutes
Director: Robert Altman Photographer: Paul Lohmann
  (Panavision & colour)
Screenplay: Alan Rudolph, Robert Altman from Arthur Kopit's play
Indians
Music: Richard Baskin
Leading players: Burt Lancaster, Paul Newman, Joel Grey, Kevin
McCarthy, Will Sampson

VICTORY AT ENTEBBE (1976)

Wolper/Columbia/Warner (David 119 minutes
L. Wolper)
Director: Marvin J. Chomsky Photographer: James Kilgore
  (colour)
Screenplay: Ernest Kinoy
Music: Charles Fox
Leading players: Burt Lancaster, Richard Dreyfuss, Elizabeth Taylor,
Anthony Hopkins, Helen Hayes, Theodore Bikel

THE CASSANDRA CROSSING (1977)

TCF/ICP (Carlo Ponti, Lew Grade) 129 minutes
Director: George Pan Cosmatos Photographer: Ennio Guarnieri
  (Panavision & Technicolor)
Screenplay: Tom Mankiewicz, Robert Katz, George Pan Cosmatos
Music: Jerry Goldsmith
Leading players: Burt Lancaster, Ingrid Thulin, Sophia Loren, Richard
Harris, Martin Sheen, Ava Gardner

TWILIGHT'S LAST GLEAMING (1977)

Lorimar/Hemdale (Merv Adelson) 146 minutes
Director: Robert Aldrich Photographer: Robert Hauser
  (Technicolor)
Screenplay: Ronald M. Cohen, Edward Huebsch from Walter Wager's
novel *Viper Three*
Music: Jerry Goldsmith
Leading players: Burt Lancaster, Richard Widmark, Charles Durning,
Melvyn Douglas, Joseph Cotten, Paul Winfield

THE ISLAND OF DR MOREAU (1977)
Cinema 77/AIP (John Temple-   98 minutes
Smith, Skip Steloff)
Director: Don Taylor   Photographer: Gerry Fisher
                                     (Movielab Color)
Screenplay: John Herman Shaner, Al Ramrus from H.G. Wells's novel
Music: Laurence Rosenthal
Leading players: Burt Lancaster, Michael York, Nigel Davenport,
Barbara Carrera, Richard Basehart, Nick Cravat

GO TELL THE SPARTANS (1978)
Mar Vista (Allan F. Bodoh,   114 minutes
Mitchell Cannold)
Director: Ted Post   Photographer: Harry Stradling Jr
                                     (CFI Color)
Screenplay: Wendell Mayes from Daniel Ford's novel *Incident at Muc
Wa*
Music: Dick Halligan
Leading players: Burt Lancaster, Craig Wasson, Jonathan Goldsmith,
Marc Singer

ZULU DAWN (1979)
Samarkand/Lamitas (Nate Kohn)   117 minutes
Director: Douglas Hickox   Photographer: Ousama Rawi
                                     (Panavision & Technicolor)
Screenplay: Cy Enfield, Anthony Storey
Music: Elmer Bernstein
Leading players: Burt Lancaster, Peter O'Toole, Simon Ward, Denholm
Elliott, Nigel Davenport, John Mills

CATTLE ANNIE AND LITTLE BRITCHES (1979)
Hemdale/Monday (Rupert Hitzig,   96 minutes
Alan King)
Director: Lamont Johnson   Photographer: Larry Pizer (CFI
                                     Color)
Screenplay: Robert Ward, David Eyre
Music: Richard Greene
Leading players: Burt Lancaster, Rod Steiger, Amanda Plummer, Diane
Lane, John Savage

ATLANTIC CITY (1980)
Ciné-Neighbor/Selta Films-EK   105 minutes
(Denis Héroux)
Director: Louis Malle   Photographer: Richard Ciupka
                                     (colour)
Screenplay: John Guare
Music: Michel Legrand
Leading players: Burt Lancaster, Susan Sarandon, Kate Reid, Hollis
McLaren, Robert Joy

LA PELLE (1981)
Opera/Gaumont (Renzo   131 minutes
Rosselini)
Director: Liliana Cavani   Photographer: Armando
                                        Nannuzzi (colour)
Screenplay: Robert Kotz, Liliana Cavani from Curzio Malaparte's novel
Music: Lalo Schifrin
Leading players: Burt Lancaster, Claudia Cardinale, Marcello
Mastroianni, Alexandra King

MARCO POLO (1982)
RIA (Vincenzo Labella)   10 hours
Director: Guiliano Montaldo   Photographer: Pasqualino de
                                        Santis (colour)
Screenplay: David Butler, Guiliano Montaldo, Vincenzo Labella
Music: Ennio Morricone
Leading players: Burt Lancaster, Ken Marshall, Denholm Elliott, John
Gielgud, Anne Bancroft, John Houseman

LOCAL HERO (1983)
Enigma-Goldcrest/TCF (David   111 minutes
Puttnam)
Director: Bill Forsyth   Photographer: Chris Menges
                                        (colour)
Screenplay: Bill Forsyth
Music: Mark Knopfler
Leading players: Burt Lancaster, Fulton Mackay, Peter Riegart, Denis
Lawson, Peter Capaldi, Jenny Seagrove, Jennifer Black

THE OSTERMAN WEEKEND (1983)
TCF (Peter S. Davis, William N.   105 minutes
Panzer)
Director: Sam Peckinpah   Photographer: John Coquillon
                                        (De Luxe Color)
Screenplay: Alan Sharp from Robert Ludlum's novel
Music: Lalo Schifrin
Leading players: Burt Lancaster, Rutger Hauer, John Hurt

LITTLE TREASURE (1985)
Tri-Star/Vista (Herb Jaffe)   95 minutes
Director: Alan Sharp   Photographer: Alex Phillips
                                        (Metrocolor)
Screenplay: Alan Sharp
Music: Leo Kottke
Leading players: Burt Lancaster, Margot Kidder, Ted Danson

SCANDAL SHEET (1985)
ABC TV/Fair Dinkum (Roger   95 minutes
Birnbaum)
Director: David Lowell Rich   Photographer: Jacques R.
                                    Marquette (Keylite PSI Color)
Screenplay: Howard Rodman
Music: Randy Edelman
Leading players: Burt Lancaster, Pamela Reed, Lauren Hutton, Robert
Urich, Max Wright

ON WINGS OF EAGLES (1986)
NBC TV/Scherick/Taft (Lyn   225 minutes
Raynor)
Director: Andrew V. McLaglen   Photographer: Bob Steadman
                                    (CFI Color)
Screenplay: Sam B. Rolfe from Ken Follett's book
Music: Laurence Rosenthal
Leading players: Burt Lancaster, Richard Crenna, Paul LeMat, Esai
Morales

TOUGH GUYS (1986)
Silver Screen/Bryna/Touchstone   102 minutes
(Joe Wizan)
Director: Jeff Kanew   Photographer: King Baggot
                                    (Panavision & De Luxe Color)
Screenplay: James Orr, Jim Cruikshank
Music: James Newton Howard
Leading players: Burt Lancaster, Kirk Douglas, Eli Wallach, Charles
Durning, Alexis Smith

BARNUM (1986)
CBS TV/Robert Halmi (Davis J.   95 minutes
Patterson)
Director: Lee Phillips   Photographer: Reginald Morris
                                    (TVS Color)
Screenplay: Michael Norell
Music: Charles Gross
Leading players: Burt Lancaster, Hanna Schygulla, Sandor Raski, Patty
Maloney, Michael Higgins

SINS OF THE FATHERS (UK TITLE: FATHERS AND SONS) (1986)
Bavaria Atelier/Bernhard Sinkel   240 minutes
(Jorn Schroder, Helmut Krapp)
Director: Bernhard Sinkel   Photographer: Dietrich Lohmann
                                    (colour)
Screenplay: Bernhard Sinkel
Music: Peer Raben
Leading players: Burt Lancaster, Julie Christie, Tina Engel, Bruno Ganz,
Dieter Laser

THE BETROTHED (I PROMISSI) (1987)
Information unavailable

CONTROL (1987)
Alliance/Films Ariane (Franco   90 minutes
Cristaldi)
Director: Guiliano Montaldo   Photographer: Armando
     Nannuzzi (colour)
Screenplay: Brian Moore, Piero Angela, Guiliano Montaldo, Jeremy
Hole
Music: Ennio Morricone
Leading players: Burt Lancaster, Ben Gazzara, Kate Nelligan, Kate
Reid, Ingrid Thulin

ROCKET GIBRALTAR (1988)
Columbia/Ulick Mayo Weiss (Jeff   100 minutes
Weiss)
Director: Daniel Petrie   Photographer: Jost Vacano (Duart
     Color)
Screenplay: Amos Poe
Music: Andrew Powell
Leading players: Burt Lancaster, Suzy Amis, Patricia Clarkson, Sinead
Cusack, John Glover

THE JEWELLER'S SHOP (1989)
PAC/RAI/Alliance/IMP (Mario   90 minutes
Bregni, Pietro Bregni)
Director: Michael Anderson   Photographer: Franco di
     Giacomo (colour)
Screenplay: Mario di Nardo, Jeff Andrews from Karol Wojtyla's play
Leading players: Burt Lancaster, Daniel Olbrychski, Ben Cross, Olivia
Hussey, Andrea Occhipinti

FIELD OF DREAMS (1989)
Carolco/Universal (Lawrence   106 minutes
Gordon, Charles Gordon)
Director: Phil Alden Robinson   Photographers: John Lindley,
     Ricky Bravo (De Luxe Color)
Screenplay: Phil Alden Robinson from W.P. Kinsella's book *Shoeless Joe*
Music: James Horner
Leading players: Burt Lancaster, Kevin Costner, Amy Madigan, James
Earl Jones, Timothy Busfield, Ray Liotta

PHANTOM OF THE OPERA (1990)

Saban/Scherick (Ross Milloy)　　　180 minutes
Director: Tony Richardson　　　　Photographer: Steve Yaconelli
　　　　　　　　　　　　　　　　(CTI color)
Screenplay: Arthur Kopit from his own play based upon Gaston
Leroux's book
Music: John Addison
Leading players: Burt Lancaster, Charles Dance, Teri Polo, Ian
Richardson, Andrea Ferreol, Adam Storke

Picture Credits

Some of the illustrations in this book come from stills issued to publicize films made or distributed by the following companies: Bavaria Atelier, Carter De Haven, Columbia, Contemporary, Enigma-Goldcrest, Geria-Lorimar, Hecht-Lancaster, Hecht-Hill-Lancaster, Heroux-Kemeney-ICC, Horizon, Lamitas-Samarkand, Mar Vista-Spartan, MGM, Norma, Paramount, Pax, Rusconi-Gaumont International, Seven Arts, Steloff-Howard-Major, Titanus, 20th Century-Fox, United Artists, Universal-International, Wakefield Orloff, Warners.

Pictures are reproduced by courtesy of the Stills, Posters and Design department of the British Film Institute, Derek East and Hilton Tims.

Although every effort has been made to trace present copyright holders of photographs, the author and publishers apologize in advance for any unintentional omission or neglect and will be pleased to insert the appropriate acknowledgement to the company or individual concerned in any subsequent edition of this book.

Index